SIGNIFICANT ARCHITECTURE

IN THE HISTORY OF

MINNEAPOLIS

by

Professor Donald R. Torbert

Photographs by

Mr. Eric Sutherland

A report of the Minneapolis Urban Design Study,
a joint study by The Minneapolis Planning Commission and the Minneapolis Chapter, American
Institute of Architects

Minneapolis, Minnesota, 1969

<u>Mayor</u>
Arthur Naftalin

<u>City Council</u>
Dan Cohen, President

Lloyd C. Anderson	Richard M. Erdall
Mark Anderson	Joe Greenstein
Vern Anderson	Gerard D. Hegstrom
Mrs. Gladys S. Brooks	Albert J. Hofstede
Jens Christensen	Rovert W. MacGregor
Richard T. Curtin	Byron F. Nelson

<u>City Planning Commission</u>
William Holbrook, President

Frank E. Adams	Robert P. Janes
Richard T. Curtin	Arthur Naftalin
George S. Hage	Mrs. Magnus Olson
A. J. Helland	Peter Woida

FOREWORD
____

This is a report on significant historic buildings and structures in Minneapolis.

A city to be distinctive must have personality. The personality of a city depends upon the natural and cultural resources in its environs. Historic buildings form a vital part of the cultural resources. Embodied in these buildings are the past history of the city, the creative expression of sensitive architects and the sentimental attachment of the people. Historic buildings provide a sense of diversity which is increasingly difficult to find in the city today.

Minneapolis is not as heavily endowed with significant historic buildings as are some older eastern cities. Many of the older buildings in the city were torn down long before World War I. Those few that remain are more precious to the city than ever.

Many of the buildings selected have outlived their economic lives. They are now threatened by demolition. Unless there is a general awareness of the significance of these buildings, the chance that they will survive the constant change in the city is rather slim.

We are hopeful that through the publication of this report we will be able to call the public's attention to the vital issue of historical preservation. More public discussion may be centered upon the significance of these buildings. Public support may be marshalled toward saving them for the use and appreciation of this generation and the generations to come.

Lawrence M. Irvin
Director of Planning and Development

David J. Griswold, Minneapolis Chapter
American Institute of Architects

INTRODUCTION

Eileen Power, a well-known historian of medieval society, once stated that history is not only written but also built up. Historic buildings and structures are a record of man's past activities in a geographical area. Man's creativities, skills, values, ambitions are permanently imprinted on these buildings and structures. Buildings and structures presented in this report indicate some of the activities in the city through its formative decades. This, however, is not a historic site study.[*] Historic landmarks without architectural significance have not been included here. Neither does this report attempt to include architectural representation from every style and period of the city history.[**] This is, then, a report on significant and historical architecture. Architecture here is broadly defined to include functional structures such as bridges and elevators. Sensitive architects, such as LeCorbusier, long ago recognized both the inherent beauty and vitality in these structures and their architectural value.

Christopher Tunnard has noted "As distinct from a purely commercial beehive, a living and vital city always retains some elements of the past.... If we let these examples fall in the path of expansion we are not only demolishing an important part of our visual inheritance--we are putting a lower value on man himself and blighting his aspirations for the future." We fully concur with him. This is a part of our total effort toward the

---

[*] This is the subject of a report by the Minnesota Historical Society titled "A History Tour of 50 Twin City Landmarks" 1966.

[**] This was attempted by Professor Harlan McClure in his booklet "Twin City Architecture-Minneapolis & St. Paul. 1820 to 1955," New York. Reinhold, 1955.

preservation of these historic buildings in this city. Other

efforts contemplated at this moment are:

1. Exhibitions and symposia on the historic buildings survey
    at major community centers in the city to publicize and
    to review the findings in this survey.

2. A study of the required legislation toward preserving
    these buildings. A separate report will be issued at a
    later date.

We are most grateful to Professor Donald R. Torbert, of the

University of Minnesota, for the preparation of this report. We

are also indebted to the fine photographs taken by Mr. Eric

Sutherland of Walker Art Center.

In the course of the preparation of this report, we have

received many valuable comments from members of the Historical

Building Survey Advisory Committee for which we are most grateful.

They are:

> Prof. Ralph Rapson, Head
> School of Architecture
> University of Minnesota
>
> Prof. Emeritus Donald Heath
> School of Architecture
> University of Minnesota
>
> Mr. Richard Heath
> Planner and Historian
> Minneapolis Planning Commission
>
> Prof. George Winterrowd
> School of Architecture
> University of Minnesota
>
> Mr. Allan Tolbert
> Minnesota Historical Society
> (since resigned from the Society)

But the Minneapolis Planning Commission and the Minneapolis

Chapter, American Institute of Architects, are solely responsible

for the contents of this report.

> Weiming Lu
> Design Coordinator

CONTENTS

<u>Illus</u>   <u>Page</u>

HISTORY

If one reads newspapers from the early decades of Minneapolis history, or the reports of growth and progress, and the city histories that appeared from time to time, it is soon apparent that many buildings once considered important and admirable are no longer extant. Because the history of the city is brief, questions arise as to what happened to these many buildings-- and why. What happened to Mendenhall's Bank, the Pence Opera, the Academy of Music and the Metropolitan Theatre, to the West Hotel, the Cyclorama and the offices of the Northwestern Miller, to the Bank of Commerce and the Guaranty Loan, to the Boston Block and Temple Court? All were once considered evidence that could be cited to prove that Minneapolis was a city of some substance, culturally aware and progressive. Some of these structures became obsolete and were razed and a few were destroyed by fire. As land values and taxes increased some were replaced by larger and more lucrative structures, others simply fell into disuse and deteriorated.

Through many years there was no strong or effective protest at the gradual, piecemeal destruction of the architectural aspect of the city's history. It seemed to be a natural and perhaps inevitable process, a price exacted by growth of the city. But as the rate of demolition increases there is a heightened awareness that real values are at stake and that the destruction which

threatens is neither good nor inevitable. It may be of some
worth to look at the nature of the city's architectural past and
to raise questions as to what should be preserved.

Superior quality of design as found in individual buildings,
even if they are widely scattered, is an obvious asset to a city,
but the architectural character and quality of the whole city or
of communities within it are determined in large measure by
factors that are more general and pervasive. Such factors are
found in the way in which the townsite is platted, the pattern
of growth as the subdivided land is developed, the attitudes and
the changes in attitude toward style, toward structure, toward
the nature and quality of building materials that occur with the
passage of time. The attitudes and practices, in regard to these
several matters, which have been characteristic of Minneapolis
through much of its history were already established and widely
accepted throughout the nation when the first permanent structures
were built at St. Anthony in 1848.

When Colonel John S. Stevens, one of the two earliest
claimants to land on the west side of the river, laid out the
original townsite for Minneapolis, legal title to the land had not
yet been granted. His survey lines were extensions of those that
had been established for St. Anthony on the east side of the river
in 1849. After consultation with other claimants to the north and
south of him, Stevens determined the pattern and orientation of
downtown Minneapolis streets by establishing Washington Avenue.
It was laid out in segments, each of which ran roughly parallel to
a section of the winding river. Each of these segments of

Washington Avenue served as a spine for a military grid of streets
and square building blocks. The straight streets were sufficiently
long to create the effect of visual corridors that lacked focal
points and ran on seemingly without termination. The military grid
system of land platting had been practical under a variety of cir-
cumstances since ancient times. It had the virtue of being easy
and cheap because it could be applied mechanically to an area of
any extent, but it devoted an inordinately large amount of land to
through-traffic streets and it took no account of the nature of
the terrain or of the widely varied human activities for which it
established the framework. In later years, when the area south of
Grant Street was platted, the grid was turned so that the streets
run due east-west and the avenues due north-south. At those
points where the streets angle sharply to the south one finds a
few of the rare spots in the city where focal points are created
by the street system. In the majority of the city's ten communities the grid forms long rectangular blocks in which the major
axis is north-south.

Well into the nineteenth century it had been the custom to
lay out a village site around a central square, greensward or open
area that was held in common. Land set aside in this way had served
as the site for a wide variety of activities and had had its
further important use in that it was the visual nucleus of the
town around which were commonly found such important structures as
the courthouse, churches, stores, inns and prominent residences.
This mode of organization gradually fell into discard as more and
more towns came into being on sites that were made up of many

relatively small holdings which continued to be exploited by their several competing owners rather than by a central authority. Minneapolis was one of many towns that never did develop a nucleus where civic life might be said to center. In the first decade of settlement Minneapolis had three areas between Bridge Square and Sixth Avenue South in each of which there was a struggle to establish a town center. From 1873 until 1914 the old city hall occupied the triangular center block where Hennepin and Nicollet Avenues converged at Bridge Square and where, in 1914, the recently razed Gateway Park was established. Even in the days when the city hall was there, Bridge Square was widely recognized as a ramshackle and dilapidated traffic corridor, not a civic center. The early landowners who gave sites for churches, a preparatory school, a park, were undoubtedly making gifts that were promotional in nature, but they were not working against the larger civic interests. Nevertheless, the competition that naturally existed among varied interests always proved to be inimical to planning and unified development. That was as true at the end of the 1880's, when the site for the present City-County building was selected with no consideration given to broad civic ends, as it had been in 1856-57 when the first county courthouse was built, as it was said, "in the brush" on Fourth Street at 8th Avenue South, an act which a newspaper of the time described as "...a cool, deliberate, unblushing betrayal of the interests of a constituency by their representatives." Neither the style nor the quality of individual buildings was determined or directly influenced by the lack of a concept of what a city should be. But failure to exercise controls and to solve civic problems in civic terms fostered uneven and

seemingly casual development that led to a central district which

is still in substantial measure curiously scattered and dispersed

and one where heavily built areas alternate with pockets of un-

occupied land, now generally used for parking lots.

Predominately residential communities, like Powderhorn and

those which border it on east, south and west, were marked by this

same uneven development through long periods. In residential areas

uneven development was most conspicuous after mass transportation

was established. While construction generally followed along the

routes of the car lines in the form of strip development, it

became feasible to skip sizeable areas. For example, Washburn Park

(in the Fuller neighborhood of Southwest Community), an area of

winding and wooded streets extending on either side of Nicollet

Avenue from 50th Street to Minnehaha Creek, was subdivided and

developed in substantial measure in the late 1880's, while a section

of the Powderhorn Community immediately south of Franklin Avenue--

from Pleasant Avenue on the west to Stevens Avenue on the east--

remained a relatively undeveloped pocket for many years after it was

platted, then became the site of some fine mansions.

In the exclusive neighborhoods where there was a clustering of

truly large and elaborate residences the development again tended to

be along a strip rather than over an area. In the Loring Park

neighborhood mansions were concentrated on adjoining Clifton,

Groveland and LaSalle Avenues. Immediately to the south, in the

Whittier neighborhood of Powderhorn Community, there was a small

area of mansions on West Franklin, Pillsbury and Blaisdell Avenues

and on short stretches of both West 22nd Street and East 22nd
Streets. The largest group of fine homes on a major street was on
Park Avenue between 22nd and 28th Streets. With few exceptions, it
was only on Park Avenue that the mansions were placed on sites
adequate for their size. Outside of Central and Powderhorn
Communities, mansion building was almost entirely confined to
Groveland Terrace, Mt. Curve and Logan Avenues in the Lowry Hill
neighborhood and to parts of the boulevards surrounding the major
lakes on the west side of the City. There were very few areas in
the City where the mansion was more than a block or two removed
from the ordinary upper-middle class house.

CENTRAL COMMUNITY

The boundaries of the city at the time the two towns of
Minneapolis and St. Anthony were incorporated as one in 1872 were
well beyond the limits of the built-up area. That part now called
the Central Community was the whole of the city which had developed
on the west bank of the Mississippi after the mid-century. The
Central Community is presently defined as bounded on the north by
Plymouth Avenue, on the northeast by the Mississippi River, on the
east by Fourteenth Avenue South and Hiawatha Avenue, on the South
by Franklin Avenue and on the west by Lyndale Avenue. On the north
the land falls away slightly. At the southwest it terminates in
the still sharply defined Lowry Hill at the base of which is Loring
Park with its small lake, but in general the terrain is flat and
featureless. It was because the early settlers anticipated the

growth of an industrial city based on the power that could be harnessed at the Falls of St. Anthony that claims were staked, and focal points for early settlement were near the anticipated industrial area along the river bluff, and along the extreme lower reaches of the military road (Hennepin Avenue) that angled off to the southwest along a route the Indians had used as approach to the point where they crossed the river at Nicollet Island.

In 1872 the Central Community was only spottily settled but it already contained the currently accepted version of most of the wide variety of building types found in the modern metropolis. Any consideration given to the question of what the Central Community is to become should start with recognition that from the early days it has been characterized by diversity and dispersion that were destructive of urban character. It was never marked by consistency in terms of structural quality, scale or visual character.

In recent years many firms have left the Central Community to locate in outlying districts, but in 1968 as in the 1870's, it is the center for retail trade, for transport, business and banking interests, for the professions and for major elements of the wholesaling and distributing trades. It still contains major elements of the city's grain storage facilities, flour-milling industry and other types of processing and manufacture. Contained within it are three major railroad yards. Along its southern border there are the remnants of two residential areas, the once elegant Loring Park Neighborhood on the west and the older Elliot Park Neighborhood to the east. As general city-center and area that still contains much multiple-unit housing, the Central Community is ill-equipped in

terms of the physical and visual amenities provided by plazas,
parks and recreational areas. The only open spaces of any substance are Loring and Elliot Parks, both toward the periphery of
the Community.

UNIVERSITY COMMUNITY

The University Community, because of its history, its physical
and cultural diversity, is one of the most complex in the city. As
it developed originally, University Community lay entirely on the
east side of the river, but the limits have recently been re-defined
to include the Riverside neighborhood on the west bank. In this
area of some 3000 acres the terrain is generally flat except for
the sharply defined river gorge and the hilly Prospect Park
neighborhood at the extreme southeast corner. On the east bank
segment, a rough triangle, community limits are established on the
north above Nicollet Island and by Second Avenue Northeast and East
Hennepin Avenue, on the east at the city limits and to the west by
the Mississippi. West of the river the Riverside neighborhood
limits are determined by the freeways, on the south at Ninth Street
South, on the west at Fourteenth Avenue South. Parts of those
neighborhoods east of the river were platted as townsites in 1849
and saw considerable settlement several years before lands
belonging to the military reservation west of the river were legally
opened for settlement. As noted, St. Anthony Falls developed on the
east bank as Minneapolis developed on the west.

Until 1872, when St. Anthony and Minneapolis--each having
several thousand inhabitants--were amalgamated, each maintained an

independence that was sometimes jealously guarded. Except for buildings devoted to functions of government, St. Anthony like Minneapolis developed the full range of residential, cultural, commercial and industrial structures that would be found in any independent city of the time and region. From the days of earliest settlement, St. Anthony contained a commercial district that extended along the part of the river frontage near the bridge to Nicollet Island and along Central and East Hennepin Avenues. Although the Falls often were cited in terms of their drama and beauty, they were the power-site and were treated as such. As severe weather and logging operations were destructive of the lip of fractuous stone that forms the Falls, it soon proved expedient to allow the beauty to be substantially covered over by a protective wooden apron. For many years, on the east side as on the west, the cities found that their commercial reason-for-being continued to center on the river area at and near the Falls of St. Anthony.

Despite the considerable diversity of interests within the area, the community takes its name from the fact that since 1856 it has been the major structural element and administrative center for the now widespread University of Minnesota. It is the extension of the several hundred acre East Bank Campus across river, to a West Bank Campus that will contain an additional fifty-three acres, that has caused the old Riverside neighborhood to be included within this community. Although Riverside was not a part of the original Minneapolis town plat, the neighborhood was settled early and for well over a generation large parts of it have been conspicuously run-down. Now in process of re-constitution, this historically old segment of the city will become one of the most consistently re-built areas. Containing as it does both major parts of the University facilities and the Campus of Augsburg College--along with the Fairview and St. Mary's Hospital complexes---the University Community will continue to be an important intellectual and cultural center. It can be foreseen that the neighborhoods on the east bank, like that on the west, will undergo rapid change. The park and recreational facilities of the community have long been inadequate and community character is not likely to be enhanced by the extension of freeways through an area already bisected by major traffic routes, railroads and a railroad marshalling yard. Many of the interesting structures built in this old area are no longer extant, a majority of them destroyed long before the freeway and the parking lot had come into being, but the University Community is still, within the context of Minneapolis architecture, relatively rich in structures worthy of conservation. Among these, several need immediate attention if they are to survive. A substantial body of University Community residents, conscious of the problems that beset the area and well aware of its history and its assets, have formed themselves into a community improvement association that energetically works to direct and control the changes that are inevitable and to see that demolition is neither wanton nor unnecessary.

NORTHEAST COMMUNITY

Northeast, immediately to the north of University Community, covers some 5400 acres and is largest in point of size of the city's ten communities. From south to north it extends from East Hennepin Avenue to the city limits at 37th Avenue N.E. Bounded on the west by the Mississippi it extends to the city limits on the east. Northeast is like the University Community in that it contains both quite old and newly developed areas. Only the southern half was within the city limits established in 1872 but the annexations of 1883 and 1887 saw the whole of the present area incorporated. The Old St. Anthony neighborhood at the southwest corner was platted in 1849 and settled in the early days but the northerly part of Waite Park neighborhood was not settled until the nineteen-fifties. The six well-defined neighborhoods of Northeast Community are bisected by railroads and by a strip type commercial district that developed along the path of the mass transit system. Northeast terminates at northwest and southeast in two of the city's largest industrial districts. The terrain is high and rolling, particularly toward the north and northwest.

Among Minneapolis communities, Northeast has an uncommonly large amount of open area in the form of playgrounds, parks, golf courses, parkways, and cemeteries. From the period of early settlement the area attracted unusually large numbers of European emigrants--Polish, German and Scandinavian--who tended to cluster in ethnic groupings. In these areas the cultural institution was, and in large measure is, the church. Except on and near the parkways, where very substantial houses have been built in the course of the last thirty years, residences are modest, generally well maintained and architecturally non-descript. In an occasional church structure there are clues to the national origins of the congregation, but these structures too are not distinguished by high quality of architectural design. If they were to be preserved beyond their natural span it would be by reason of the strong affection of their parishioners rather than because they represent true architectural distinction. Even the design of the brewery of the early nineties at Marshall and Broadway lacks the romantic extravagance, now again considered attractive, of many nineteenth century breweries. The Shoreham Shop of the Soo Line Railroad on Central Avenue N.E., designed by Kenyon and Maine in 1912, is perhaps still the strongest design in the Community.

POWDERHORN COMMUNITY

The Powderhorn and Central Communities are contiguous along Franklin Avenue which is the northern boundary of one and the southern boundary of the other. The eastern limit of Powderhorn is established by the diagonal of Hiawatha Avenue, that on the south through most of its length by 42nd Street, while the limit on the west is defined by 2nd Avenue South between 42nd and 36th Streets and by Lyndale Avenue between 36th Street and Franklin Avenue. Within this area there are nine residential neighborhoods along with extensive business, industrial and institutional properties. The physical character of the extensive Powderhorn Community is even less varied than that of Central Community. The high ground of the Loring Park neighborhood extends south into

Whittier neighborhood on the extreme northwest corner of the area.
Aside from that, the only marked variance in the terrain occurs
within Powderhorn Park where the land drops sharply to create the
bowl-like slopes that surround the small lake. Although there are
several recreation fields, inadequate in size and too widely
separated, the only park-like area aside from Powderhorn Park it-
self is the wooded square of Fairoaks Park on which the Institute
of Arts faces.

Small areas that constitute a strip along the northern edge of
Powderhorn were incorporated into Minneapolis in 1867, 1872, and
1881, but the major part of the acreage between Franklin Avenue and
38th Street was brought into the city in 1883 and the remainder,
lying between 38th and 42nd Streets, was incorporated in 1887. As
was true of the Central Community, Powderhorn was built up spottily,
sporadically and over a period of several decades. Before the most
southerly parts had filled-in in the 1920's the older areas to north
and east were deteriorating. Although the commercial and industrial areas within Powderhorn Community are conspicuous and un-
attractive they occupy less than ten percent of the land. Half of
the nearly 4000 acres are devoted to housing units, some two-thirds
of which are in the form of two-or-more-family units. Some thirty
percent of the land is occupied by streets and alleys. Industry is
confined to the 28th-29th Street Crosstown Strip which parallels
the tracks of the Chicago-Milwaukee-St. Paul and Pacific Railroad
that were carried across the city in 1884. Another railroad and
industrial complex begins immediately at Hiawatha Avenue, the
boundary between Powderhorn and the Longfellow Community to the

east. Commerical development, largely of the strip type, occupies substantial frontage on Franklin Avenue, 26th and 28th Streets, and the entire length of Lake Street. Commercial development also has invaded major north-south avenues--Lyndale, Nicollet, Fourth, Park, Chicago, Bloomington--most thoroughly between Franklin Avenue and Lake Street. In the area north of 26th Street and terminating on the east with Park Avenue, the community contains such important cultural institutions as The Minneapolis Institute of Arts and Minneapolis School of Art, Hennepin County Historical Society, the American-Swedish Institute, and the remains of several of the city's finer residential streets. Here again is that proximity of old and new, of the dilapidated and the carefully maintained that is seen in some degree in each of the communities. It is nowhere more marked than in the extensive area of Powderhorn.

NEAR-<u>N</u>ORTH <u>C</u>OMMUNITY

The Near-North Community, bounded by Lowry Avenue on the north, the Mississippi River and Lyndale Avenue on the east, Plymouth Avenue and the Great Northern Railroad tracks on the south and by the city limits (France Avenue, Theodore Wirth Park and Xerxes Avenue) on the west, is like the Northeast community in that it contains areas of widely diverse quality that range from very poor in the east and central neighborhoods to excellent along part of the western limits. That part of the Community not within the limits of the city as incorporated in 1872 was annexed in 1883. Contained within it are two major industrial areas, railroads and railroad yards and, again, the community is bisected by several heavy traffic arteries. In Near-North Community the areas adjacent to the Mississippi tended to be settled first and to be attractive to industry. The early development, in the 1870's, was followed during the economic boom of the eighties by the extension of transit lines and more widespread settlement.

In Near-North there were two residential pockets that took advantage of the wooded and irregular terrain to break with the rectangular block mode of ground platting. In the mid-eighties, Oak Park Addition in Grant neighborhood and Forest Heights Addition in Lowell neighborhood, like the contemporary Prospect Park in University Community and Washburn Park in Fuller neighborhood of Southwest Community, were laid out with curved tree-lined streets. These residence park areas in Near-North, like the later highly restricted Homewood Addition in western Hay neighborhood, were never fully successful in their attempts to be exclusive. From the eighties on down to the present day, home owners of upper middle-class economic status have been drawn increasingly west and south, toward and beyond the lakes and Minnehaha Creek. Only the western limits of Near-North, with considerable areas of park and playground and close proximity to Theodore Wirth Park, have maintained the air of a select residential area. The greater part of the 3500 acres in Near-North were fully developed by 1915 and all but the area along the southwestern limits was built-up by the early-thirties. The older sections of Grant and Harrison-Glenwood neighborhoods, marked by widespread deterioration, are the site of extensive redevelopment.

Near-North, like Northeast and the Riverside neighborhood of

University Community, was attractive to ethnic and religious
groups--German, Scandinavian, French, Finnish, Russian-Jewish,
Polish--who formed cohesive neighborhood settlements through long
periods but left surprisingly little by way of distinctive mark on
the architecture of the areas where they lived, that little of
doubtful significance.

CAMDEN COMMUNITY

Camden extends from Lowry Avenue north to the city limits at
53rd Avenue and from the Mississippi on the east to the city limits
(Victory Memorial Drive and Xerxes Avenue) on the west. Within the
bounds of these 3300 acres there are seven residential neighborhoods, a large cemetery, a long industrial strip along the river
from which railroad tracks cut across to the Soo Line switching
yards and an adjacent industrial area. Despite railroad and industrial areas Camden is predominently a residential community of
pleasant, small, single family residences of no special distinction,
the majority of them built since 1920. Chief among the visual
amenities of the area, which is rolling to the south and flat to
the north, are the broad, tree-lined parkway of Victory Memorial
Drive, which passes through the area east to west then turns south
to form a major segment of the Community's western boundary, and
the parked recreational area bordering on Shingle Creek which cuts
diagonally across the northern half of Camden. There were a few
settlers and a shingle mill near the river front in Camden before
the mid-nineteenth century, but the whole area was brought into
the city with the annexations of 1883 and 1887. It was in the

boom period of the eighties and, in particular, in the decade of the nineties that Camden became of central importance to the then great lumbering industry. In 1890 Minneapolis was the lumber capital of the world and remained so until the turn of the century, after which time the decline was so rapid that every important physical trace of the industry disappeared within twenty years. From the physical and visual viewpoints a whole great chapter in city and regional history substantially disappeared. The lumbering industry never constituted a visual amenity, housed as it had been almost entirely in crude wood sheds of the most elementary character. Smaller industrial units and storage facilities have replaced in some degree the shingle mills, brick kilns and sawmills that lined the Camden river area in the nineteenth century. Today, Camden is seen at its best in the attractive areas along the Memorial Drive. There is little to indicate that the area had a history which has disappeared.

CALHOUN-ISLES COMMUNITY

The limits of Calhoun-Isles are established on the north by the Great Northern Railroad tracks which form the southern limit of the Near-North Community, on the east by Lyndale Avenue South, on the south by W. 36th Street (Lakewood Cemetery), Calhoun Boulevard and W. 38th Street, and by the city limits at France Avenue on the west. Of the near 2900 acres in the Community, about 700 are in the form of Lake of the Isles and Lakes Cedar and Calhoun. Taken together the three constitute about half of the total water area in the city.

Aside from the lakes, the most conspicuous feature of the terrain is the bluff of Lowry Hill. From this high ground the land falls away gradually to south and west but rises again in the southern area bordering Lake Calhoun. Considerable wooded and open terrain is found in The Parade, Kenwood Park, the boulevards and parkways that surround the lakes and in the extensive private grounds of the Minikahda Club on the high ground west of Lake Calhoun. In addition to three major residential neighborhoods there are a number of residential pockets or small, semi-isolated areas created either by the railroads that cross Calhoun-Isles, in both east-west and southwest-northeast directions, or by a short commercial-industrial strip that centers on W. 29th Street between Lyndale and Hennepin Avenues. Those avenues and Lake Street have become commercial strips.

Only the northeast corner of the area was brought within the corporate limits prior to the major annexation of 1883, at which time all of the land now contained in the Community became part of Minneapolis. Although areas around the lakes, Calhoun and Cedar in particular, had been popular spots for boating, fishing and picnics from the early days and had seen the construction of recreation pavilions and a resort hotel, the Calhoun-Isles Community developed very slowly. A few houses were built in the mid-seventies but it was not until the eighties, by which time a steam powered mass transit line had been built out to Lake Calhoun, that widespread settlement occurred. This was markedly stimulated in the later eighties by Park Board improvements of the lakes and by the early stages of development of Lake of the Isles and Dean Boulevards and a portion of Kenwood Parkway. The east side of the Community

developed rapidly between 1890 and 1915 but the area west of the

lakes was substantially settled only between 1925 and 1940 with

pockets west and south of Lakes Calhoun and Cedar completely built-

up only in the years following World War II. Calhoun-Isles, like

Powderhorn and University which also adjoin Central Community,

contains cultural institutions--the Guthrie Theatre and Walker Art

Center most notably--that are of as great significance to the city,

state and region as to the immediate surroundings. The northern

half of Lowry Hill neighborhood and the areas near the lakes, as

one would expect, have long been considered highly desirable

residential property. From the late nineteenth century until after

the Second World War these areas were sites for the construction of

some of the largest and most expensive homes--many of them handsome--

in the city. Unfortunately, with few exceptions even the splendid

among them were built on plots of inadequate size, which gives rise

to a sense of crowdedness in some residential districts where,

ordinarily, it would not be encountered. Congestion of this type

menaces a neighborhood or community most obviously when large units,

by reason of age or high cost of maintenance, become impracticable

as residential property. If and when they can no longer be used

essentially for the purpose for which they were designed it is a

near certainty that the effect on the neighborhood will be

deleterious--no matter how worthy the purpose for which they are

used. Before the westerly and most recently developed parts of

Calhoun-Isles Community had filled-in, the east half had become

sadly altered in character, the central, parkway strip of trees replaced by street railway tracks in what had been the Hennepin Parkway and many of the old mansions converted to rooming houses, apartments and commercial purposes.

LONGFELLOW COMMUNITY

Across the city to the east and again adjoining Powderhorn is the 2900 acres of Longfellow Community where the relative flatness of the terrain is relieved by the gorge of the Mississippi and by lesser gorges and ravines in and around Minnehaha Park. On the north, Longfellow adjoins the Riverside neighborhood of University Community at the freeway, Interstate 94. On the east and south are the river and Minnehaha Park. To the west, Longfellow terminates in the Hiawatha Avenue industrial strip. North of Franklin Avenue, as along the western boundary, Longfellow is heavily commercial and industrial and, in addition, is bisected by the Lake Street commercial strip.

Part of the extreme northerly section of Longfellow lay within incorporation limits as established in 1856, in 1867 and 1872, but it was the annexations of the eighties that brought the whole of the present Community within the city. Here again actual settlement took place over a long span of years. The first extensive development, in the seventies, followed the construction of the Milwaukee Railroad line that parallels Hiawatha Avenue, but Longfellow also contains the newest single-family residential development in the city on the West River Road south of Michael Dowling School from 40th to 42nd Street. Actual settlement thus covers a period of some ninety years but the major part was

accomplished between 1895 and 1930 and was closely related to the
growth of transit facilities and stimulated by Park Board
acquisitions and improvements that occurred most notably in 1889
(Minnehaha Park) and in 1902-05 (West River Road Park). Longfellow
is a predominently residential community of owner-occupied single-
family dwellings. Because of the parks that bound it to the east
and south, much of the area is pleasant, but, excepting Saarinen's
Christ Lutheran Church, little of the building is artistically
significant. In the park area, a considerable historic interest
attaches to the John Stevens cottage (the first house on the west
river bank site of Minneapolis) of 1849, the Carpenter-Gothic
Minnehaha railway station and the Soldiers' Home.

SOUTHWEST COMMUNITY

Despite the fact that a tendency to move toward south and west
was already evident in the eighties, substantial areas in the most
southerly communities, although annexed in 1887 and 1927, have been
developed only in recent years. Southwest Community is large, near
to 5000 acres, and extends from West 36th Street and Calhoun
Boulevard on the north to the 62nd Street Crosstown Expressway on
the south, from Interstate Highway 35W (Stevens Avenue) on the
east to the city limits, France and Xerxes Avenues on the west.
The outstanding physical amenities in this generally high quality
residential area of nine neighborhoods are Lake Harriet and
Minnehaha Creek which bisects the Community, west to east, south of
the lake. The extensive area west from King's Highway to Linden
Hills Boulevard and south from Calhoun Boulevard to the north

shore of Lake Harriet is one of the most highly developed park
areas in the city--containing Lyndale Park and rose gardens, Lyndale
farmstead (administrative quarters for the Park Board), Lakewood
Cemetery and, on the north shore of Lake Harriet, a marshland,
wildlife sanctuary. Minnehaha Parkway, opened in 1893, swings
south and east from the lake.

The earliest evidence of settlement in the area was the Sioux
Indian School of 1835 on the west side of the lake. That, like the
large residence on Colonel William S. King's 1400 acre Lyndale Farm,
of 1870, is no longer extant. Soon after the extensive annexations
of the eighties a few houses were built near the lake but growth was
relatively slow until the boom period of the twenties when much of
the area north of 54th Street was filled in. Except for extended
commercial strip development along Nicollet Avenue and the northerly
and southerly sections of Lyndale Avenue, the principal commercizl
properties are in the form of a few relatively well contained
neighborhood shopping areas. Near the extreme southeast corner of
the Community there is one small industrial pocket served by a
spur-line railroad. In recent years many apartment houses have been
built but as late as 1960 83% of the housing was in single-family
units and almost 80% of all housing was owner occupied. On the lake
boulevards and adjacent streets, as on the parkway, there are many
fine residences and the Community also contains a number of churches
that often are carefully designed but rarely carried out in a contemporary architectural spirit. Two of the most interesting are
Bethlehem Lutheran at Lyndale and 41st Street and the considerably
older Byzantine Chapel, by Harry Jones, in Lakewood Cemetery. The

few structures once in Southwest that might arouse interest by
reason of their history are no longer extant; structures of high
quality now there are little menaced by reason of age or unstable
surroundings. The most conspicuous landmark in the attractive old
Washburn Park area of Fuller neighborhood is Washburn Water Tower.
Whether, with the passage of time, it will become the object of
aggressive, protective affection--like that lavished on the long
unused tower on Tower Hill by the residents of Prospect Park in
University Community--remains to be seen. In many cases, only
that kind of aroused Community spirit can save a threatened
landmark.

NOKOMIS COMMUNITY

Nokomis, again with an area of some 5000 acres, is second
largest among the city's ten communities. It is bounded on the
north by Powderhorn at 42nd and 43rd Streets, on the east by
Hiawatha Avenue and Minnehaha Park, to the south by the city limits
at the 62nd Street Crosstown Highway and Metropolitan Airport and
on the west by Interstate 35W (Stevens Avenue).

The outstanding physical feature of Nokomis is the substantial
area of water in Lakes Nokomis, Hiawatha, Diamond, Pearl and
Mother. the last named, at the south limit of the area, is sur-
rounded by extensive marshland which is a bird and wildlife
sanctuary--one of two areas of virgin land within the city. The
Community is bisected west to east by Minnehaha Parkway and there
is virtually no industry in the area.

The three neighborhoods south of 54th Street were annexed in

1927, all of the land to the north having been incorporated in
1887. Until about 1920 Nokomis developed slowly, only those
neighborhoods on the north being served by transit lines on
Minnehaha, Chicago and Fourth Avenues South. Park Board
acquisitions and major improvements around the lakes in the years
following World War I stimulated settlement south of the parkway
and development was rapid after 1920. Over 90% of the housing
units in Nokomis are single-family dwellings and 88% of all
housing is owner-occupied. There are many fine homes on the parkway and around Lake Nokomis but they are not buildings of real
architectural distinction. The best known structure in the
Community is the much admired 'Fish' Jones house (now Longfellow
Branch Library) at Minnehaha Parkway and Hiawatha Avenue. It is
not, though it is widely believed to be, a true scale replica of
the historically significant, mid-eighteenth century, Vassal-
Longfellow house at Cambridge, Massachusetts. It is presently
marked for demolition in the course of highway construction.

In the several brief reviews of community development and
character given above, the words--bisected by railroads--crossed
by heavy-traffic routes--industrial districts--strip commercial
development--settlement along transit lines--development long-
drawn-out--were repeatedly employed. No one of these factors can
be said to determine absolutely the character or the quality of
design found in an area's buildings. However, in combination or
alliance with the attitudes toward architectural style and

structural quality, toward land usage and property rights, that
have prevailed throughout the nation during the period of
Minneapolis' history, they have helped bring into being a city
which, despite its amenities, is unpleasantly diverse visually
and woefully lacking in urban character. For that, no one factor
is more clearly responsible than is the concept of architectural
style manifest through much of that period of history.

STYLE
____

Among the several aspects of architecture that influence the
visual character of an environment, style is the most obvious. In
the course of the increasingly eclectic 19th century, styles were
borrowed, chosen full-formed, rather than developed. Neighborhoods
that came into being over the course of relatively few years were
characterized by marked architectural variety. Stylistic differences more often were manifestations of changing fashion than of
basically changed concepts of what a building should be. The
differences that one notes among a group of contemporaneous houses
or business buildings arose out of whim, out of the vagaries of
taste. Because none of those manifestations were indigenous, had
real roots in the region, the surface characteristics that were
accepted as style were subject to frequent change. At any one
time, later nineteenth century building may be marked by such
variety of stylistic differences that the elements from several
sources form a melange, an eclecticism of personal taste. In the

course of less than a century no fewer than fifteen fashions had varying degrees of influence on Minneapolis buildings, and that number is not inclusive of the always quantitatively important vernacular "plain building" or of occasional sporty forays into such exotica as the Moorish, Chinese or Egyptian. While it is true that styles came and went, it is also true that after the Classic Revival and the Gothic Revival were established there was never a time when some form of classicized and some form of medievalized architecture were not being designed. The fashions came into being in a known order but thereafter they were not so much a simple sequence as a concurrence with considerable periods of overlap. The earliest true Revival movements--Classic and Gothic--had their origins in the eighteenth century in an era of craft economy and skilled craftsmen builders that, in every essential respect, had come to a close by the time Minneapolis was settled. The standards of excellence found in the early years could not be maintained, a fact of great importance to quality of design in the later nineteenth century.

Thomas Jefferson introduced the Classic Revival in the United States in 1789 when he made use of a Roman temple as the basis for his design for the Virginia State capitol at Richmond. A decade later Benjamin Latrobe used a Greek portico on his Bank of Pennsylvania at Philadelphia. From that time there was increasing interest in the Greek but the severe mass, austere forms and heavy columns that are seen in the best Greek Revival architecture in the course of the forty years after 1820, played no part in Minneapolis architecture. Traces of Greek Revival "influence," as it could be seen in numerous Carpenter's Guides and Handbooks, are found in the cella-block form of the carpenter vernacular houses, in enframed doorways that carry a wooden entablature and in cornices and frieze boards that carry across the ends of the building to form pedimented gables with raking cornices. Many such houses were built at Minneapolis before the Civil War and they were to be found in considerable numbers only fifteen years ago. There are faint traces of such influence in buildings like the Godfrey Cottage of 1848 in Southeast Minneapolis, but few are known to remain. Awareness of Roman temple forms was to be found in parts of the format and in details of such early structures as Old Main at the University, of 1856, but that too no longer exists.

The early phases of the Gothic Revival occurred in England at the middle of the eighteenth century and in the United States a half-century later. Latrobe adopted the style in 1805 for the project design he first submitted for the Roman Catholic Cathedral in Baltimore. That project was rejected in favor of a classicized design by the same architect, but interest in the style developed and soon other American "classicists" designed Gothic Revival churches. Gothic educational buildings were designed as early as 1814 and by 1832 a taste for the fashion had emerged in the field of domestic buildings. In the early period of Minneapolis' history there were both Carpenter Gothic cottages, as early as 1851, and Carpenter Gothic churches. In many examples the Gothicism consisted of little more than steeply pitched roofs and jig-sawed or molded wood tracery along the eaves. The style was less widely accepted than were the simpler classicized or vernacular forms.

Designs of the favored type were widely known through inclusion in A.J. Davis' Rural Residences of 1837, A.J. Downing's Cottage Residences of 1842 and the small church designs of Richard Upjohn. The best example of the cottage that remains in the city is the much altered house built by B.O. Cutter at Fourth Street and 10th Avenue S E. in 1856. In the Central Community the only example is a church, once interesting but now altered beyond recognition. It was the Swedenborgian Church of the New Jerusalem, of 1869, which is at Ninth Street and 5th Avenue South.

The third of the fashions to be noted in Minneapolis was the Tuscan or Italian Villa which was not a true revival of an earlier Italian style. The originals for this type of design were the architectural remains pictured in the landscape paintings of Claude Lorrain and Nicolas Poussin. In the late eighteenth century, British romantics gave real substance to these concepts. By 1830 the type appeared in this country in a so-called Tuscan house by Town and Davis, and in a villa described in a publication by A.J. Davis in 1835. Downing's 1842 edition of Cottage Residences contained ten designs of which four were Italianate. It was a flexible mode of design, there being no canon of proportion associated with it. It could be symmetrical or asymmetrical in plan. In either case, it was covered with a roof of very low pitch which was frequently hipped. The much extended eaves were supported by brackets, often elaborately turned or scroll-sawed. The effect that was generally desired could be attained through ornament applied to a carpenter vernacular building. Elaborate examples of the type often were L-shaped in plan and carried a square tower at the inside angle of the L. In simpler versions the villa was a rectangle without a tower, its most conspicuous feature the eave brackets and low-pitched roof. In that form it was often referred to as the Bracketed style. Italianate houses were popular in Minneapolis from their introduction in the fifties until the late seventies. Again, the most fully developed examples of the type have been razed, but Italianate influences are seen in the Woodbury Fiske and Thomas Andrews houses from 1869-70 on 5th Street in Southeast Minneapolis.

During the first phase of the Gothic Revival there was also a taste for Romanesque forms, in particular for details and usages adopted from the German Romanesque. These were admired in eastern cities where one might see Romanesque industrial buildings, railroad stations and churches, as well as residences. The fashion appears never to have had substantial influence in Minneapolis, but traces are seen in early photographs of the now much altered stone church of 1857 at 21 Prince Street Southeast. Now known as Notre Dame de Lourdes, it was built by the Universalists. The paired, elongated round-headed windows and the semi-circular chancel were evidences of the taste for the Romanesque.

The use of French Neo-Baroque approaches to design, as revived under Louis Napoleon, constituted the major high-style of the third quarter of the century. The mansard, double-pitch, or curb roof appeared along the east coast even before 1850. This roof form, in many variations, along with the elaborated dormer windows that accompanied it, were the outstanding feature of the Second Empire style. In expensive examples the walls simulated the effects of

light and dark that were the consequence of having been designed
"in depth," a practice not characteristic of American building in
general and one that was quite foreign to the vernacular. The
many variations on these Second Empire themes undoubtedly were
drawn from a variety of sources, but the best known work was that
of Visconti and LeFuel who, in the years 1852-57, made extensive
additions to the Louvre for Napoleon III. An American book that
made the style available in the provinces was <u>Villas</u> <u>and</u> <u>Cottages</u>
published in 1857 by Calvert Vaux. Vaux recommended the mansard
for practicality as well as for style and illustrated several
varieties of the elaborate, heavy archivolts and over-windows that
were widely favored. The earliest mansard known to have been used
in Minneapolis was on the Samuel Gale residence of 1864. Through
the following twenty years it was extremely popular, used in every
type of building and every size of structure from Crown Roller Mill
to modest residences. Of this widely favored style virtually
nothing remains in Minneapolis; a representative example from 1872
is seen in the Governor Alexander Ramsey house on Exchange Street
in St. Paul.

Many works that were characteristic of the city in the early
decades are no longer extant because they were on property that
became valuable and the early structures were replaced, but much
building was never worthy of architectural interest simply because
it was tawdry. Newspapers from the eighteen-eighties like those
from the eighteen-fifties make repeated references to vulgarity of
design and shoddy construction. Much of the ornament, whether used
in modest or lavish amounts, was jig-sawed or made of sheet metal,

cast iron or cast stone and was applied with nails to thin-wall structures. The ornament tended to rust, peel, warp, curl, rot--and being tacked on, tended to fall off. A share of the shoddiness was to be accounted for by low-budget building but much was due, though not from necessity, to the mode of construction that was employed. In all but the largest masonry buildings the balloon frame was used. It served the need for speed and economy, and the services of skilled craftsmen were not essential but the light, wood frame was not well adapted to the realization of styles that had been developed in masonry during earlier periods of history. It had been the advent of the high-speed power saw, which made it possible to cut thin dimension-lumber very rapidly, together with the invention of machinery which, unattended, cut building nails from wire, that made the balloon frame possible. The modular framework of two by fours could be quickly sheathed with clapboard or covered with a veneer of brick or, on occasion, stone. This thin-wall construction was the means most often employed in building even in the heart of the Central Community until, in the eighteen-eighties, the institution of safety laws and the establishment of an office of Building Inspector encouraged a measure of care in construction. Tall commercial and industrial buildings were necessarily of solid-wall construction. The steel or ferro-concrete framework and the curtain wall were not used in Minneapolis until the turn of the century.

Almost as soon as Carpenter-Gothic churches ceased to be built about 1870, Gothicism was resurgent in a somewhat changed form that was used for schools and business buildings as well as in churches.

Gothic houses were not popular in the seventies and eighties, the taste for the Gothic being expressed primarily in a generalized emphasis on verticality, in the use of patterned and vari-colored slate roofs and in a liking for white stone trim in contrast with strong-red brick walls. These buildings were neither copies from known structures nor taken directly from the ample literature on the fashion, but they appear to have had their sources in English work rather than American. The churches, now larger than in the earliest period and more substantially built of brick or stone, were derived more directly from published designs by men like G.E. Street and Sir George Gilbert Scott than from those of Americans like Richard Upjohn or James Renwick. The added element in the medievalism of the eighties was the arcaded Venetian Gothic which had been made known to Americans through the literary and critical works of the much admired John Ruskin. The single re-maining example in Minneapolis, not a noteworthy design, is the Chute Building designed in 1881 by W.H. Dennis and located at East Hennepin and University Avenues Southeast.

The so-called "Queen Anne" style, which supplanted the Victorian phase of the Gothic, was not a true revival but an eclectic compound from its inception. The British architects linked most closely with the origins of the Queen Anne were Eden Nesfield, Norman Shaw and Philip Webb. Gothicists in their early work, these men developed into architects who incorporated motifs from a wide range of sources into their, for that time, regularized plans and simplified facades. Shaw, best known among them, would use Tudor bays and half timbering and Dutch Renaissance and Flemish Baroque gables along with doorways, white-painted sash windows and low relief carving which he adopted from vernacular "Classic" work of eighteenth century England. As motifs borrowed from the Classical tradition came to play a more dominant role in the fashion, Queen Anne merged into the melange called Free Classic. In America, Queen Anne-Free Classic buildings were decidedly not simple in composition. The style name, familiar after about 1877, came to mean "anything goes." Its visual quality is perhaps suggested by the fact that a well known architect dubbed it the Bric-a-brac style. In England, J.J. Stevenson and E.R. Robson made their versions of Queen Anne popular for large public and commercial buildings. All of this was reflected in the Minneapolis of the eighties where designs for large and important structures like the West Hotel and the Tribune Publishing Company, as well as those for numerous residences of pattern-laid shingles or of shingle and brick, took full advantage of the almost unlimited design scope allowed the architect. The pattern-laid shingle buildings that Harry Jones designed for the Park Board, now much altered or destroyed, were attractive local examples, as was his old Minnetonka Yacht Club. Queen Anne became a catch-all name used to cover the most irrationally individualistic designs of the period. All of the important examples have been razed or altered almost beyond recognition.

By the time H.H. Richardson's 1874 design for Trinity Church of Boston was completed in 1877, the architect had become famous throughout the country. His style, not too aptly known as Richardsonian Romanesque, made use of elements taken from remains

in Early Christian Syria, from Romanesque France and Spain, and
from France of late Gothic and Renaissance times. In Richardson's
best work all of that was subjected to the control that marked his
distinctly personal sense of style and conditioned by his sensibility to scale and proportion. The great majority of his many
followers appear to have been impressed only by massiveness, by
heavily worked stone surfaces and by the way Richardson used an
arcade of great round-headed arches to link the openings of several
stories into one design motif. Richardson's sensitivity to the
qualities inherent in materials was most unusual in his time as
was his capacity to simplify complex designs. The best qualities
in his work were not easily imitated, but his style had a powerful
effect on many American cities that were undergoing rapid growth in
the period of prosperity that extended from the late eighteen-
seventies to the early eighteen-nineties. In Minneapolis the
Richardsonian influence was important but of brief duration, lasting
from 1884 to the early nineties. After the turn of the century an
occasional design was to reveal that its author had profited from a
study of Richardson's works. Of the numerous important civic
structures, commercial buildings, banks, churches and mansions
built in a Richardsonian manner in Minneapolis very few remain.
Only two are essentially unchanged in appearance, Long and Kees'
City-County Building of 1889-1905 and Buffington's (Harvey Ellis)
design for Pillsbury Hall of 1888 at the University. Both are
landmarks in the city's history. The style did not survive the
years of depression subsequent to 1892 or the increased interest in
academic architecture which became evident again in the late

eighteen-eighties and was widely popularized by the Chicago World's
Columbian Exposition of 1893.

A flurry of interest in French Renaissance design, inspired by
the work of Richard Morris Hunt, was contemporaneous with the Queen
Anne and Richardsonian Romanesque. French Renaissance was not the
sole approach to design favored by Hunt but it was one well adapted
to use in the homes of the very rich, for which purpose it was
employed with some frequency from the time Hunt initiated the vogue
in a Vanderbilt mansion in New York, in 1878, to his design of
1890-95, of the vast country retreat Biltmore, near Asheville, North
Carolina, for another Vanderbilt. From the standpoint of the
client, French Renaissance design was admirably suited to the purpose of extravagant display. In terms of historic connotations,
the style was a symbol of wealth and power. But, for America at
large, it had distinct limitations in that the forms were not
designed for effective translation into wood, the style depended
on a wealth of carved detail and derived a large part of its
character from the use of extravagantly soaring roofs, of turrets
and stair towers. In Minneapolis the influence of the style was
confined almost entirely within the brief period 1887-1893. Extant
examples, none of them distinguished, are to be seen in the William
Channing Whitney design for the Merrill residence of 1887 on East
22nd Street at Second Avenue South, in a group of linked town
houses, "Zier Row," designed by W.H. Dennis in 1889 for Fourth
Avenue South at Ninth Street, and in a crude but flamboyant example
in the Van Dusen residence which Orff and Joraleman designed in
1892 for 1900 LaSalle Avenue.

Not all designers and not all owners were committed to the use of extravagant or fanciful decorative devices. Even when the taste for the unusual was at its height, many saw the virtue of a comparatively straightforward no-nonsense design wherein appearance resulted substantially from the way in which openings were distributed and in which materials were used. This approach, often favored in Chicago in the years following the great fire, came by 1880 to be called "Chicago Commercial." The name did not mean that all traces of the architectural past were avoided---simple cornices, moldings, string courses, arched windows were commonly used, but the name did carry the connotation of a building fabric free of superficial, romantic features. Only commercial building was referred to by the name, and it varied from very bad to very good in design. The six-story, stone Hayer Building at Third Street and Third Avenue North is the best building of the type to survive in Minneapolis' Central Community.

Well before all of the fashions outlined above had ceased to interest designers and clients, both the classicizing and medievalizing forces were resurgent in somewhat new guises. Great dissatisfaction with the state of the nation's architecture had been expressed as early as 1876 when the centennial of our independence had helped focus attention on our Colonial past and its building. In 1877, Robert Peabody of Peabody and Stearns in Boston had voiced the thought that the least artificial revival for this country would be one based on our Colonial building. In that same year members of the Boston Architectural Club made a pilgrimage to parts of New England for the specific purpose of seeking our own past.

Out of this new temper, and probably out of sheer weariness with much that had been done in later times, there developed a renewed interest in Georgian or so-called Colonial, Italian Renaissance, Roman and, again, Baroque forms. In 1883 the McKim, Mead and White offices turned to the Italian Renaissance City Palace as source material when they designed the Villard houses at 50th Street and Madison Avenue in New York. In 1886 the same firm used American Georgian, of a type more familiar in Virginia than in New England, as the source for the H.A.C. Taylor house at Newport, and classic elements again shaped their design of the Boston Public Library in 1888. In these same years lofty business buildings were caused to carry richly detailed classic cornices far above the street, while Palladian windows and arcades of round arches resting directly on columns were brought into widespread use. Well before the Columbian Exposition at Chicago in 1893, this latter-day classicizing was well-launched and had found a receptive public at every economic level where there was any interest in architecture.

The span of years that had elapsed between the introduction of a fashion in the east and its appearance in Minneapolis was now much reduced. By 1888 Minneapolis architect Harry Jones had built a Georgian house, "based on" the Longfellow house at Cambridge, for a client on Elmwood Place in Washburn Park. In the same year Babb, Cook and Willard of New York built the ten story, red-brick and white stone, Renaissance style New York Life Building, now razed, on Second Avenue South. In 1891 Farmer's and Mechanic's Bank erected a Roman Temple as their new banking house at 115 South Fourth Street. That facade, as extended and altered in 1908, now serves as street front for Schiek's Restaurant. Virtually every type of building except that for heavy industry was affected, and quickly, by the new interest in Classicism.

Throughout several decades American architects gave lip service to the merits of those several styles that, taken together, constitute the classic tradition, but in practice, scant respect was paid to the factors that determine quality of design. In the great majority of cases the Classic heritage was treated as nothing more than an inexhaustible and presumably indestructible mine of decorative treatments and devices. In the eighties the lumber companies had already commenced the manufacture and stock-piling of Palladian window units, of Georgian and Adam dormers, of porch posts in the Orders, of stock-item entrances with side lights and fan lights, of Colonial, Georgian and Federal mantle-pieces, of dadoes, newel posts and balusters. Although the so--called Colonial house sometimes came near to authenticity in appearance, more often it was nothing but square and white with a bit of 'stock' trim. From the late eighties to the late nineteen-thirties, this classi-cizing approach was widely favored and is still, there can be no doubt, widely admired today.

In Minneapolis, buildings that affected to be more or less Greek, Roman, Renaissance, Palladian, Baroque, Georgian or American Colonial were built as banks, stores, office buildings, a railroad depot, a museum, churches and temples, theaters, schools, auditoria and, of course, as houses, in perhaps several thousands of examples. Among the houses old and new, which exist in large numbers, there are many, perhaps hundreds, that are pleasant, livable and dignified

(good local examples and that cover a substantial span of time are
to be seen at 314 Clifton Avenue, 2250 W. Lake of the Isles Blvd.,
2100 Stevens Avenue South, 2525 E. Lake of the Isles Blvd., 2100
Pillsbury and 2215 Pillsbury Avenue), but among these buildings of
all types there are few if any so unusual, so well composed, so well
proportioned or so carefully crafted that they are likely to elicit
the feeling that they should, in the public interest, be the subject
of special action directed toward their conservation or preservation.
Whatever the style, the elements which establish it are almost
always too big or too little, too heavy or too thin, too stingy or
too gross.

Even the more successful among the 'rationalized classic'
designs, such as the Soo Line Building (formerly First National-Soo
Line) at Marquette and 5th Street, designed in 1914 by Robert W.
Gibson of New York, lack the honesty and directness of the earlier
buildings for Deere and Weber (Midwest Merchandise) or Northern
Implement Co. (Pittsburgh Plate Glass). In the Soo Line the "style"
is obviously decorative rather than structural and the entire design
maintains the fiction that a tall building is analogous to a Classic
Order, or to a column, and needs division into elements that cor-
respond to those of base, shaft and capital. However, the design
avoids the ponderous heaviness characteristic of the time which
often was due to the use, at top and bottom of the building, of a
clutter of bulbous decoration in glazed terra-cotta. In fenestration and in scale of decoration the Soo Line Building moves
toward that comparative openness and lightness that make it still
congruous with, and equal in quality to, the buildings of a

generation later that surround it.

In the late eighties it was not classicized architecture alone that was the subject of renewed interest, for the Gothic too came into greater favor. This was not a second revival but a continuation with a changed focus and new stylistic emphasis. The resurgent Gothic of the nineties and later decades became more and more proper. In Minneapolis it was used primarily for residences, churches, and for an occasional special purpose building--such as the Minneapolis Club. The domestic architecture was based largely on Tudor and Jacobean prototypes. The half-timber effects, which appeared first in Minneapolis in 1893, undoubtedly owed much of their popularity to the British government exhibits that contained half-timbered country houses at both the 1876 and 1893 fairs. Houses of the type, half-timbered or not, were considered particularly appropriate on rolling or wooded sites, where they were first seen on Lowry Hill. The Collegiate Gothic taste influenced neither the University of Minnesota nor the public schools and the building of Early English Gothic churches--superficially after the "correct" manner established by Ralph Adams Cram about 1892--was not felt here until later, when the Cathedral Church of St. Mark and Hennepin Avenue Methodist were built. It was rising costs more than waning interest or growth of architectural rationalism that finally brought the Gothic to a near demise in the years after World War II. In recent years there is a strong, and understandable, tendency to condemn the nineteenth century designers of naive--now amusingly quaint--Carpenter-Gothic buildings much less heartily than even the best of those more scholarly and correct architects

of later generations who turned to the Middle Ages for inspiration.
It is an attitude that is sometimes justified, sometimes not. One
of the best of the Gothic-inspired churches in the city is the
relatively recent Bethlehem Lutheran at 4100 Lyndale Avenue South,
designed by the Lang and Raugland office in 1927. Thirty-eight
years later, in 1965, the same firm made extensive additions to
the church, additions that are modern in spirit, functionally
designed, and that blend happily in scale and material with the
earlier structure--a type of success in design that is too rarely
encountered.

In several of the phases or manifestations of fashion, much
that purported to be serious concern with style now appears to have
been concern only with whether the composition of a building would
be symmetrical and regular or asymmetrical and picturesque. In the
field of residential building, only that segment of the population
that lived well above minimal levels could afford to exercise much
choice in the matter. Taken all together, the "styled" houses
from all periods--whether Tudor, Cotswold Cottage, Italian Palazzo,
Spanish Hacienda, Norman Farmhouse, French Provincial, or the
ubiquitous American Georgian and Dutch colonial--each of which had
its day--had less overall effect on the appearance of large urban
residential areas than did the fact that the most economical way to
build was in the form of a squarish two-story house, placed on a
small lot, and sheathed with clapboard or stucco. The "bungalow"
in various guises, usually one and one-half stories in height,
became very popular in the later years of the second decade of the
century, but the dominance of the basically box-like two story

house was not affected until the advent and great popularity of
the single story so-called "rambler" in the late thirties. It has
been outlying and suburban districts, rather than the areas here
under consideration, that have been shaped by the rambler.

In all periods of growth and in practically all areas of the
city it has been the vernacular, design as understood and practiced
by the carpenter and the small contractor, that has been dominant
visually. This has not been true in the same degree or through so
long a period of time in the field of heavy-duty commercial and
industrial construction. There, influences that stemmed from the
work of thoroughly professional designers who worked or lived in
Chicago are evident from the mid-eighties. From the close of the
Civil War the increasing need for large scale, heavy-duty construction had kept some areas of the building trades in a state of
ferment. At Chicago in particular, the combination of forces
generated by the high rate of growth, cost of land, physical nature
of the city site and sub-site, and the general state of the economy
had virtually forced the more creative designers to rethink the
problems of building from foundation to roof.

Although Chicago was easily accessible to Minneapolis during
these years, the revolutionary advances in building technology that
developed there in the eighties had no effect on construction in
Minneapolis until 1900. The early evidences that Minneapolis
architects were aware of Chicago are purely stylistic and un-
related to Colonel Jenney's introduction of steel-frame, curtain-
wall construction in 1883-84. The early "Richardsonian Romanesque"
compositions in Minneapolis, as, Long and Kees' Corn Exchange

Building of 1885 at 404 South Third Street (razed), used materials and motifs in ways that are more characteristic of John Wellborn Root of Chicago than of Richardson himself. That is again true in Long and Kees' rock-faced stone Lumber Exchange Building of 1885 at Fifth Street and Hennepin and of Harry Jones' National Bank of Commerce (razed) of 1888. It was Richardson's own widely scattered work, however, that was direct source material for the old library (razed) of 1886, and of the aforementioned City-County Building and Pillsbury Hall at the University. The best of these buildings that reveal the influence of the "Chicago School" are a little later, and give evidence in greater or lesser degree of their designer's consciousness of Louis Sullivan.

The Sullivan influence, which might in several, but not all, examples equally well be called Richardson-Holabird and Roche-Sullivan influence, appears as early as 1892-93 in an isolated example, but is seen primarily between 1900 and 1910. Aside from the Flour Exchange at 310 Fourth Avenue South, designed and erected through four stories in 1892-93 but not constructed in the upper seven stories until 1909, and the Grain Exchange of 1900-1902, at Fourth Street and Fourth Avenue South, these several buildings were warehouses and warehouse-assembly plants built along or near railroad sidings. Buildings such as the Grain Exchange of 1900-1902, Deere and Weber of 1902, Advance Thresher and Emerson-Newton Plow Co. of 1900 and 1904, Pittsburgh Plate Glass of 1910---all by the firm of Kees and Colburn, and Butler Brothers of 1906-1908 by Harry Jones, vary from elaborately detailed to austerely simple, but all are rigorously severe when compared with designs for the

Radisson Hotel and Donaldson Medical Building (altered) of 1909-10,
both of which carried large amounts of ponderously heavy and over-
scaled "classic" ornament in terra cotta. The limited popularity
of the simpler, more unitary, designs was due perhaps to their lack
of that excess which the period identified with opulence and
"richness." The several severe or reserved designs cited above
are not equal in the quality of their design, but they are
characterized as a group by massiveness, clear organization,
simplicity, clean silhouette, and by the suppression of subsidiary
or incidental detail. In these matters they are easily dis-
tinguishable from more historically oriented contemporaneous
buildings of equally sound structure--as seen in the Wyman-
Partridge Building of 1896 at First Avenue North and Fourth Street,
the Andrus Building of 1898 at 512 Nicollet Avenue, the Security
(Midland) Bank (now resurfaced) of 1905-06 on Second Avenue South
at Fourth Street or the Soo Line Building of 1915 at Marquette and
Fifth Street.

After 1910 the current of design that was relatively independent of borrowings from history--and which by that time could be
called the Sullivan-Wright approach to design---was confined almost
entirely to the area of residential architecture. The chief ex-
ponents of that approach were partners in the firm of Purcell and
Elmslie, who built a number of handsome residences in the city
between 1908 and 1917; their one Minneapolis church, the cubiform
original section of Stewart Memorial Presbyterian, at Stevens
Avenue and Thirty-second Street, obviously was inspired by Wright's
Unity Temple at Oak Park, but it is not equal in terms of quality

or consequence to the Wright design.

Structures of substantial size, as they were built in the downtown area in the years of prosperity after 1922, continued to favor the use of historically based ornament--classic or gothic-- in "rationalized" or emasculated forms which became even more lifeless as they became less gross. The new element in the architecture of the downtown area in the twenties was the use of the stepped tower as a form for business buildings. While the office building in the form of a campanile, tower or spire is found as early as 1873 in R.M. Hunt's design for the Tribune Building in New York City, it was the dramatically tall examples such as Ernest Flagg's Singer Building of 1909 and Cass Gilbert's Woolworth Building of 1909-13 that captured a wide audience. Further acceptance of the stepped-tower form for high buildings was stimulated by the adoption in 1916 of a zoning law in New York City which prescribed the amount of the base area of the building which could be used at varying heights above ground level. The Rand Tower of 1929, with ornament based on the highly stylized floral motifs popularized by the Paris Exposition of Decorative Arts of 1925, and the Northwestern Bell Telephone tower of 1932-34, with its nervously angular and bald "machine-age" decorations, were the major as they were the terminal essays of the type in Minneapolis.

By any architectural standards known to the twentieth century, the Foshay Tower of 1929 would be a sport even in a period much given to incongruous alliances. The peculiar form of the Foshay stems from the fact that a business building was cast in the guise of a symbol and was meant to be a memorial, a monument. More than any other building in the central area it appears to be "the Minneapolis building people remember." As such, it probably should be judged by whatever standards are appropriate or applicable to public curiosities, rather than by those appropriate to architecture proper.

From the early thirties through the immediate post-war years, buildings in the Central Community were enlarged, re-sheathed and remodeled, but there was virtually no construction of large new buildings until the mid-fifties. Such construction of sizable works as was carried on tended to be outside the central area until 1955, when the long familiar so-called International Style--a framework sheathed with a thin curtain or membrane of glass or metal panels--was used by Perkins and Will in their Lutheran Brotherhood Building at Second Avenue South and Seventh Street. That was followed at the end of the decade by the steel, aluminum and glass sheathed slab that Holabird, Root and Burgee (Thorshov and Cerny associated) designed for the First National Bank at Second Avenue South and Fifth Street. The two structures are unfortunately pedestrian and unexciting designs when compared either with the Skidmore, Owings and Merrill Lever House at New York of 1950, or with Louis Sullivan's Carson-Pirie-Scott Building at Chicago of 1899, or again--with the General Mills headquarters building of 1958 on Wayzata Boulevard.

In the extensive Longfellow Community, there is one building of "modern" persuasion which needs to be mentioned in this context of modern architecture. Longfellow community is marked by great natural beauty in the parkway area along the river bluffs and in

Minnehaha Park proper, as noted above, contains interesting me-
mentoes of the past in the form of early mill sites that ante-
date permanent settlement outside the fort and now contains the
cottage Colonel John S. Stevens erected on his claim near St.
Anthony Falls in 1849, the small, wood Minnehaha rail station and
the Old Soldiers' Home, but the entire community's one truly distinguished building is Christ Lutheran Church, of 1949-1950 by
Eliel and Eero Saarinen, at 3244- 34th Avenue South. Christ
Lutheran, along with contemporaneous structures by Saarinen in
Indiana and Michigan, had an important and continuing influence on
the character of church architecture in this and other cities.

The struggle to bring a meaningful, modern architecture to the
community--in residences, churches, schools, business buildings--
had been carried on with some success and for some years before
large downtown structures were erected, by, among others, the firms
of Close and Close, Karl Graffunder, David Griswold, Ralph Rapson,
Magney, Tusler and Setter and Thorshov and Cerny. But up to the
time when the Gateway redevelopment project was initiated it was
these large buildings that, to the general public, represented
what was new among the many approaches to building that could be
found in the center of the city.

On the pages above that are devoted to style and to attitudes
toward architecture, the comments relative to a particular style
often terminated with the statement that virtually nothing remains
from this period or aspect of our city's past. Whatever the reason
for their demise, many of the buildings and building types that

would ordinarily be considered for preservation because of their
priority in point of time, or because of historic associations,
no longer exist. Substantial parts of this destruction occurred
before World War I--it is in no sense a phenomenon to be observed
only in recent years. The early or original examples of the
following buildings, normally the subject of architectural interest
and effort at the time of construction, are no longer extant or are
altered beyond redemption:

> THE CITY HALL
>
> COUNTY COURTHOUSE
>
> FEDERAL COURT BUILDING
>
> UNIVERSITY "OLD MAIN"
>
> SCHOOLS, PRIOR TO THE MID-SEVENTIES
>
> NINETEENTH CENTURY RAILRAOD TERMINALS
>
> THEATRES
>
> AUDITORIA AND OPERA HOUSES
>
> EARLY WHOLESALE HOUSES
>
> MILLS AND MANUFACTORIES BUILT BEFORE 1879
>
> THE GRAIN EXCHANGE
>
> CHURCHES PRIOR TO 1883
>
> BANKS PRIOR TO 1891
>
> THE PUBLIC LIBRARY
>
> EARLY HOTELS
>
> PUBLISHING BUILDINGS AND INSURANCE BUILDINGS PRIOR TO 1890
>
> WITH RARE EXCEPTIONS, AND MOST OF THOSE IN SOUTHEAST
> MINNEAPOLIS, THE RESIDENCES OF EARLY SETTLERS AND OF
> FAMILIES WHO CAME TO PROMINENCE IN THE EARLY DAYS HAVE
> NOT SURVIVED.

As in other cities of the later nineteenth century, growth was never controlled by a commonly held concept of what the city ought eventually to be. Town as economic environment appears always to have been given more thought and attention than town as social environment. The random growth that was permitted if not fostered by casual, laissez-faire attitudes now complicates the problem of restoration and preservation in that such interesting buildings as do survive usually stand as isolated examples in areas that are, on the whole, not worthy of special attention. There is no sizable area or district, no "old town," of shabby but sound buildings which gas lights and Victorian color schemes can restore to life. This does not mean, of course, that the preservation of fine, or of merely typical, buildings should not be pursued, but it presents a different kind of problem than that encountered in cities that contain within them the remnants of an architectural Golden Day.

CRITERIA

Quite beyond the area of economic considerations, three different kinds of argument may be brought to bear in support of a building's conservation or preservation; they belong to the realms of esthetics, history and sentiment. While no building should be expected to register high on all three scales in order to be adjudged worthy, the ideal building for preservation would be one of superior architectural quality, of recognizable historic significance to the nation, region, or immediate locale, and it would be the object of warm regard, emotional attachment or veneration.

Such buildings do exist and in considerable number; obvious examples are Independence Hall at Philadelphia and Jefferson's home
"Monticello" in Virginia. But a far larger number that by con-
sensus would be described as having very little merit as architecture also are fully worthy of careful preservation, an example
being the Victorian Gothic water tower on North Michigan Avenue
at Chicago, which not only commemorates the great fire of 1871 but
in its architectural character evokes an era of the city's history.

Among the three bases for judgment cited above, that of
historic significance would seem to be the easiest to determine,
though historic value obviously is not the quality that is first
to be recognized or established. The historic meaning or value of
buildings is, in fact, often revealed quite slowly and in different
ways to different people. In many cases, it remains a subjective
judgment. Despite affection for and continued interest in a
variety of styles that we commonly call "Colonial," it can be said
that in matters of architecture Americans have not been history-
minded in so far as either our past or our development are concerned. We have been more inclined to commemorate that which is
lost than to conserve that which remains. We tend to ignore the
essentially social character of building. For example, while the
tremendous import of the balloon frame to the settling of the
American West was in one sense recognized in the very speed with
which the structural method was adopted, the whole matter was
sufficiently taken for granted that its actual origins are still a
matter for conjecture. Again, the origin of the late nineteenth
century "Akron Plan" churches is known and charted and many

excellent examples are extant, but appreciation of the social importance of this type of church plan for Protestant America has
been so limited that there has been no systematic or concerted
attempt to conserve or preserve the best examples of the type. In
the eighteen--eighties Warren Howard Hayes designed a number of
Akron Plan churches in Minneapolis, of which several are extant.
First Congregational Church on Fifth St. S.E. is among the better
local examples.

As a people we have not been much given to sentiment and
affectionate regard in so far as buildings are concerned. Even
those structures that have now come to be regarded as national
shrines--Independence Hall, Mount Vernon, Monticello--often were
shamefully neglected and saved from collapse or demolition only
through heroic, last-minute action on the part of a small body of
devoted conservationists. Much that should have been preserved
obviously has been lost. In Minneapolis, a very large part of the
most truly historical building must now be found in the written or
photographic record. Among the structures that are extant--what
does the general public value? What should it value? The questions
are genuine and not easily answered. As a constantly enlarging
percentage of the urban population becomes increasingly mobile it
develops no strong sense of identity with either the present of the
place in which it lives, or with its past or future. This fact
complicates every aspect--including the financial--of the problem
of conservation, but does not make it impossible of solution. Unless a broadly-based interest is developed we stand in real danger
of becoming a society which has destroyed the substance of its

architectural heritage.

Pleas for conservation or preservation on the ground of esthetic quality, of architectural excellence, are again in large part based on standards and judgments that are not absolute and unchanging. The fact that esthetic judgments are only relatively stable is evident when one considers the degree to which attitudes toward nineteenth and early twentieth century buildings that made use of forms borrowed from the past, and toward "Late-Victorian" design in particular, have changed in recent years. Monumentally scaled complexes like the Grand Central and Pennsylvania Railroad terminals at New York City, not long ago considered embarrassingly unoriginal because of their heavy debt to Imperial Rome, are today the subject of anguished outcry when they are insensitively used, as in Grand Central, or demolished, as in Penn Station. The capacity of a building to serve the functions it was built to serve, the fitness of the materials to the ends they serve, the degree to which the building can be called structurally honest--these are subject to relatively objective judgment. But proportion, scale, spatial qualities, the use of materials--these are matters of sensibility, both for the architect and for the client or spectator.

Of the several architectural styles that are associated in their fullest development with the western world, only those that lie at the core of the Classic tradition developed a rule or canon that prescribed how a structure and its parts should be proportioned. The canon for the Classic Orders, influential through long periods of time although never adhered to rigidly or mechanically, was respected and the restraint which it fostered continued to be felt in post-Renaissance times. That sense of rule, of their being a comprehensible right-way of proportioning, continued to be an influence in the Classic Revival of the later eighteenth and early nineteenth centuries, but serious revivalism of that nature played small part in the history of Minneapolis. At the core of the romanticism that came more and more to dominate the arts in the period there was the desire to be free of rule, and it was freedom from apparent rule that was one of the charms medieval architecture-- and Egyptian, Moorish, and East Indian--had for the nineteenth century mind. All styles of building, including those based on the Classical tradition, then came to be designed in terms of individual sensibility rather than in accord with prior example or established authority. And it is on the basis of sensibility to what we now consider the essentials of architecture that the designs must be judged.

BUILDINGS

The brevity of the list that follows is not meant to suggest that no other buildings are worthy of attention, respect or conservation. However, the city has never been well endowed with buildings of high quality or with structures that are rich in terms of historic associations. Again, much that might be of interest is no longer extant.

Some of these buildings clearly deserve full effort in the interest of their conservation or preservation because of superior architectural quality. Others, together with bridges and grain elevators are structures which--by reason of their nature, history, import to the community, placement, or relatively interesting architectural quality--are felt to be amply worthy of having serious attention directed to their conservation.

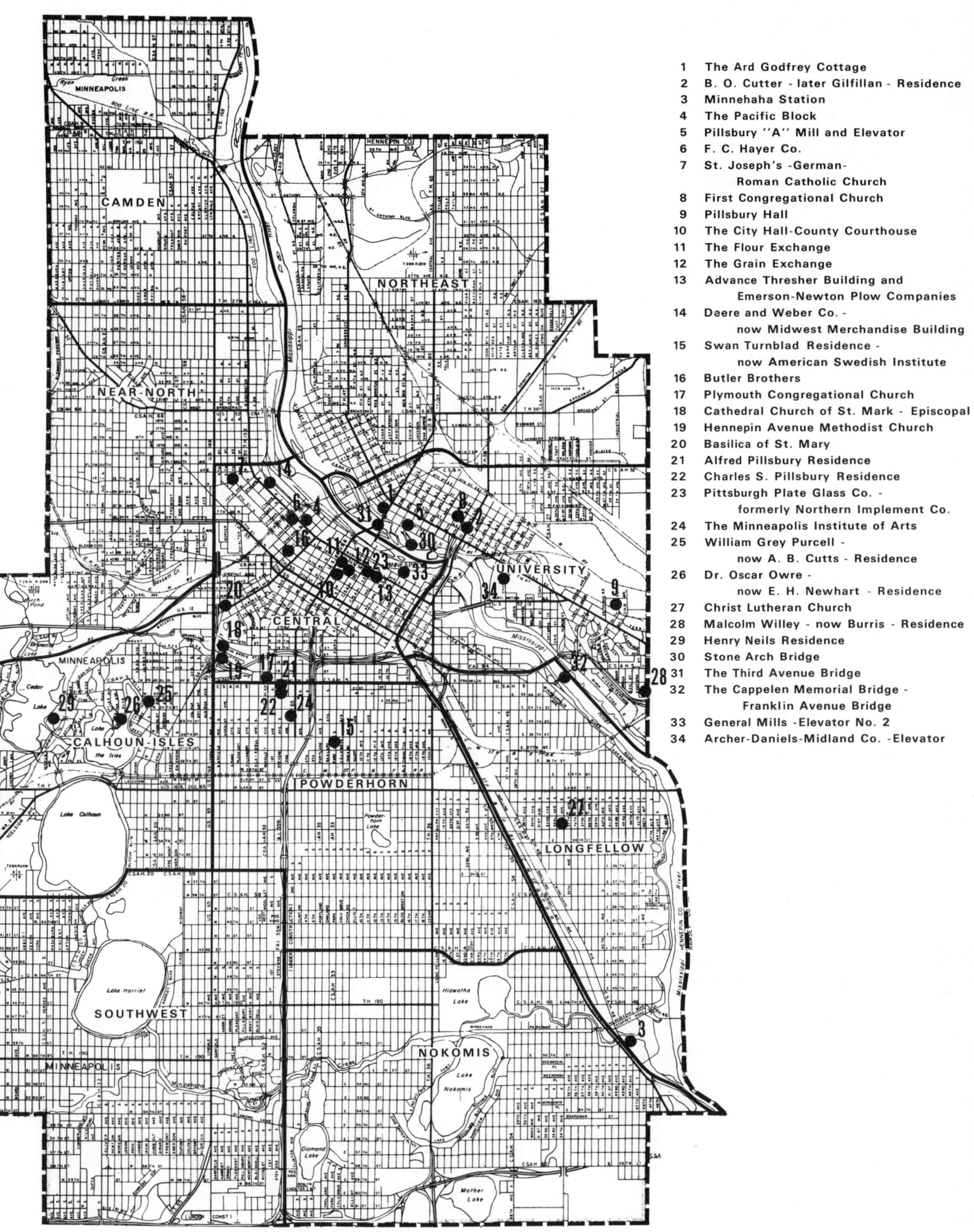

1   The Ard Godfrey Cottage
2   B. O. Cutter - later Gilfillan - Residence
3   Minnehaha Station
4   The Pacific Block
5   Pillsbury ''A'' Mill and Elevator
6   F. C. Hayer Co.
7   St. Joseph's -German- Roman Catholic Church
8   First Congregational Church
9   Pillsbury Hall
10   The City Hall-County Courthouse
11   The Flour Exchange
12   The Grain Exchange
13   Advance Thresher Building and Emerson-Newton Plow Companies
14   Deere and Weber Co. - now Midwest Merchandise Building
15   Swan Turnblad Residence - now American Swedish Institute
16   Butler Brothers
17   Plymouth Congregational Church
18   Cathedral Church of St. Mark - Episcopal
19   Hennepin Avenue Methodist Church
20   Basilica of St. Mary
21   Alfred Pillsbury Residence
22   Charles S. Pillsbury Residence
23   Pittsburgh Plate Glass Co. - formerly Northern Implement Co.
24   The Minneapolis Institute of Arts
25   William Grey Purcell - now A. B. Cutts - Residence
26   Dr. Oscar Owre - now E. H. Newhart - Residence
27   Christ Lutheran Church
28   Malcolm Willey - now Burris - Residence
29   Henry Neils Residence
30   Stone Arch Bridge
31   The Third Avenue Bridge
32   The Cappelen Memorial Bridge - Franklin Avenue Bridge
33   General Mills -Elevator No. 2
34   Archer-Daniels-Midland Co. -Elevator

The Ard Godfrey cottage   1848

Chute Square (Central Ave. and University SE.)

Designer unknown

The Godfrey Cottage was one of the earliest, if not the first,
of the houses built in St. Anthony. (The other most likely con-
tender for first-built /recently razed/ was the two-story house of
John North, also from 1848.) The story and a half Godfrey house
represents 'Classic Revival' influence reduced to its simplest
terms and become a part of the vernacular. That influence is seen
in the design of the entrance with sidelights enframed by capped
pilaster strips and surmounted by a two-member entablature, in the
pilaster strips at building corners and in the simple frieze and
cornice which are returned about three feet around the gable ends.
(The John Stevens cottage of 1849, 'first-built' on the west bank
and now in Minnehaha Park, is an even more simplified version of
the general type.)

The Godfrey house was moved from the original site on 2nd
Street SE. years ago but stands boarded-up, neglected and deteriorating on a site where it is never likely to attract much
attention. It should be moved again and rehabilitated if it is to
survive. The general type of which it is representative once
existed in perhaps hundreds of examples in St. Anthony and
Minneapolis.

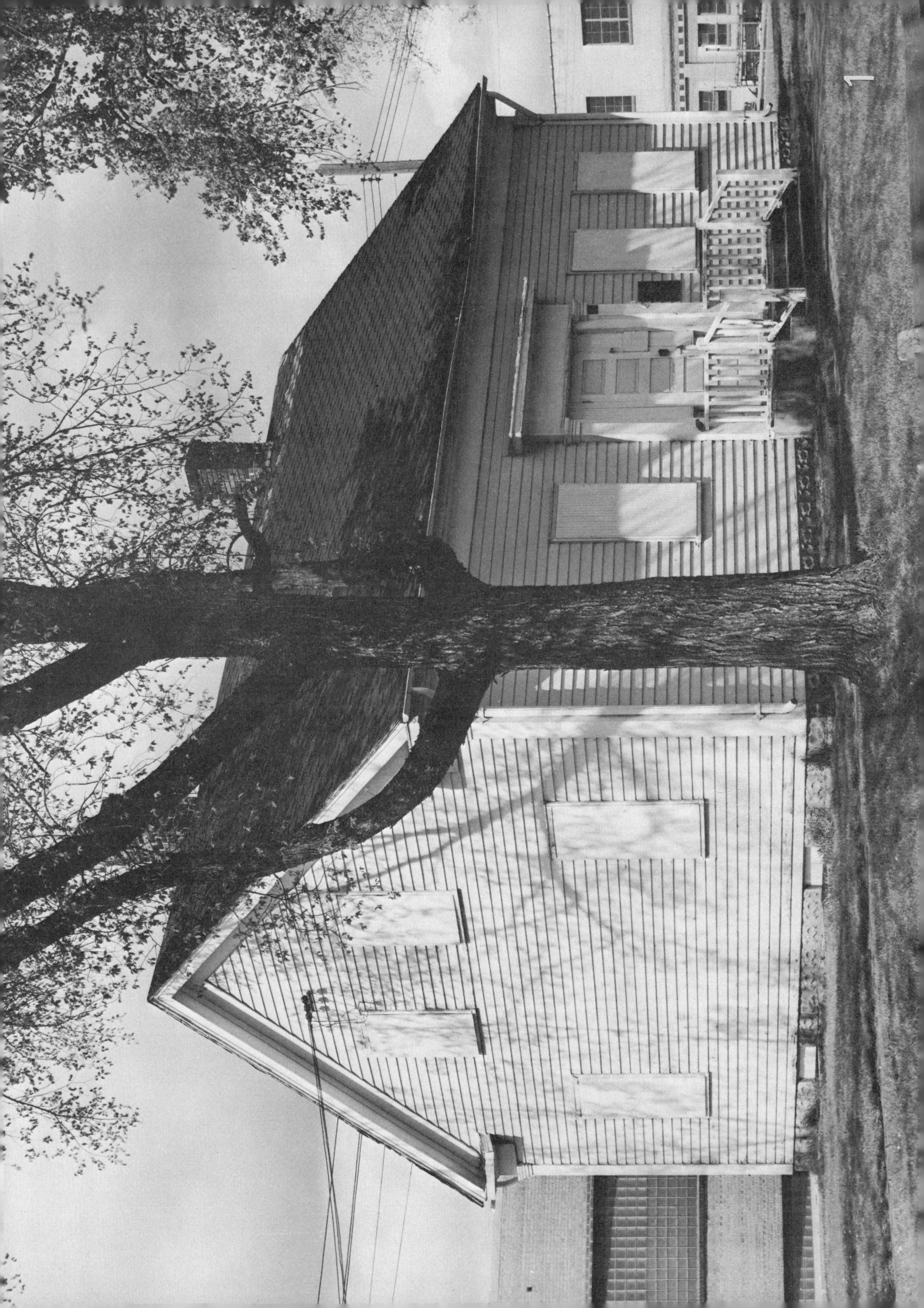

B.O. Cutter (later Gilfillan) residence   1856
Fourth Street and Tenth Avenue SE.
Designer Unknown

Cutter came to St. Anthony in 1856, as did the first archi-
tect--R.S. Alden, to supervise construction of Alden's "Old Main"
at the University. His house, much extended to the north in 1874,
was one of the most elaborately decorated of the Gothic cottages
built in Minneapolis and is the only one of this character to
survive. The several owners have given attention to retaining the
decorative features but the effects of age are now evident. The
original wall surfacing was not stucco as it has been for some
thirty years, but planks cut to resemble blocks of dressed stone
which were then covered with paint into which sand had been mixed.

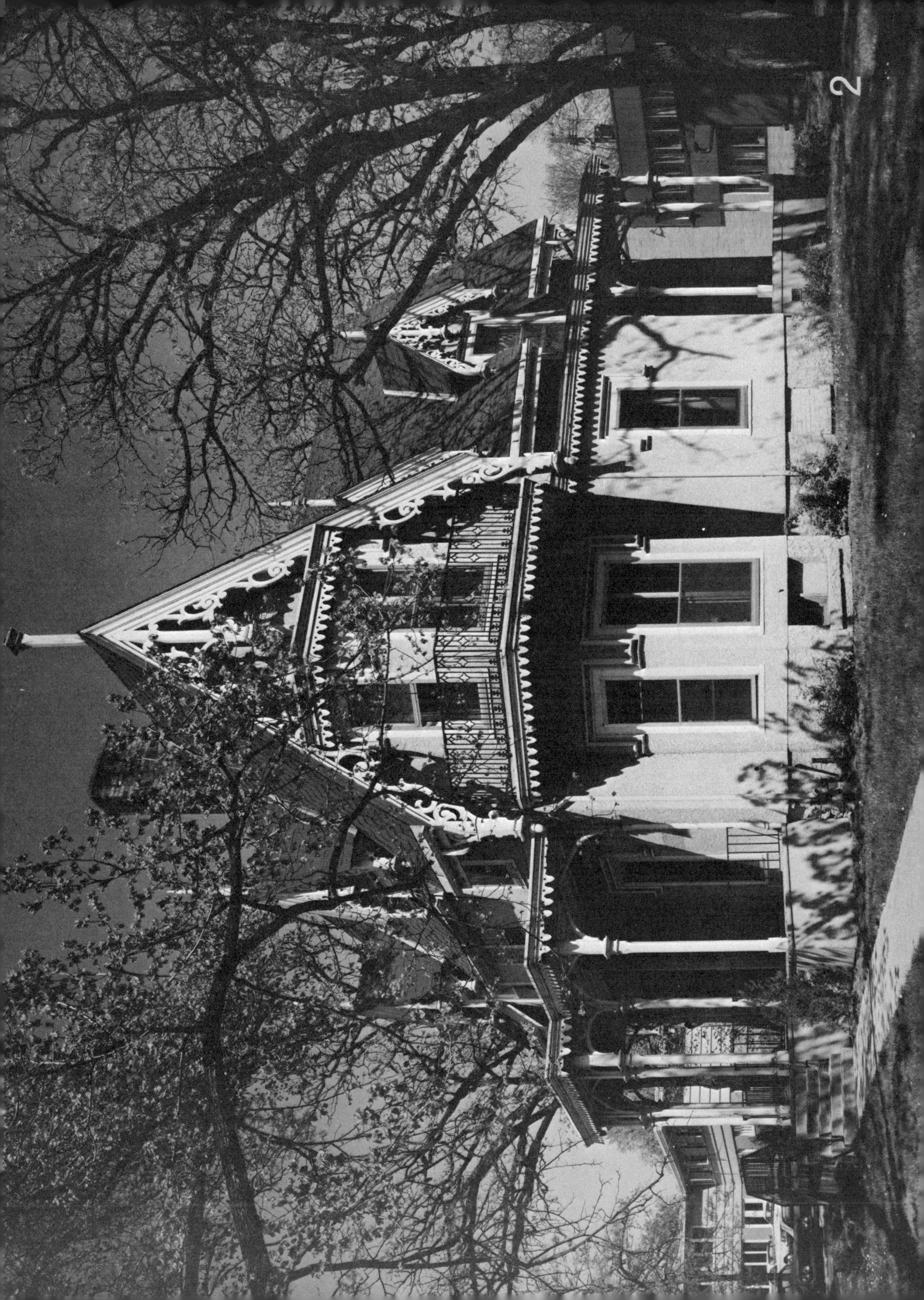

Minnehaha Station   1870's

Minnehaha Park near

42nd Ave. South

Designer Unknown

    This romantic curio, small station for a narrow gauge rail-
road, like the Cutter house is one of the few Carpenter-Gothic
or Steamboat Gothic buildings to survive. All of these structures
exploited in greater or lesser degree the design potentials of
the jig-saw and "dimension" lumber.

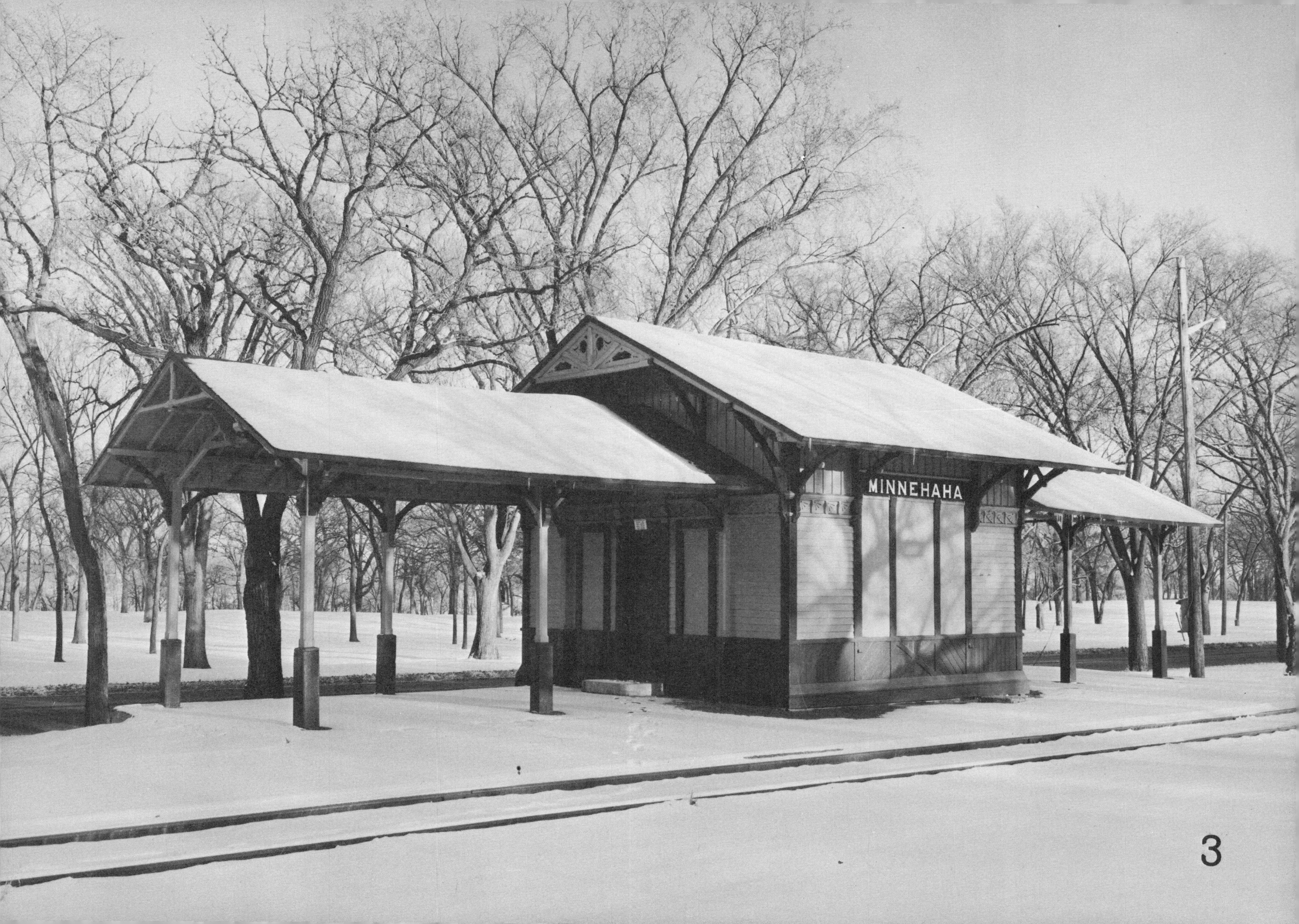

MINNEHAHA

The Pacific Block   (date uncertain)

218-228 Washington Avenue North

Designer Unknown

The Pacific, now in very poor physical condition, is a good
example of a mode of design once widely favored and now dis-
appearing very rapidly from the urban scene. From the Civil War
through the 1870's designs of this type were used for buildings
that were usually of brick and of almost every size and type from
Crown Roller Mill, on First Street at 5th Avenue South, to the
ubiquitous twenty-two foot "business front." The facades of these
buildings, and it is rather distinctly a facade architecture, are
divided into panels that commonly run the full height of the
structure. The width of the panels one might assume, on the basis
of logic, to have been determined by the spacing of bearing walls
or partitions carried at right angles to the facades. In many
examples the panels are in fact quite arbitrarily designed,
according to taste rather than to the dictates of structural
necessity. Decoration, aside from the panels and a cornice, which
was usually of wood or sheet metal and very heavy in scale, is
ordinarily concentrated on the segmental or round-arch over-
windows, caps or lintels that are, again, almost invariably
elaborate and visually heavy. Such buildings are not fine, not
even honest, but today they tend to evoke a sense of brooding
melancholy that we associate with many aspects of the period to
which they belong. It is these half-haunted facades that often
line the streets in paintings by Edward Hopper and Charles
Burchfield.

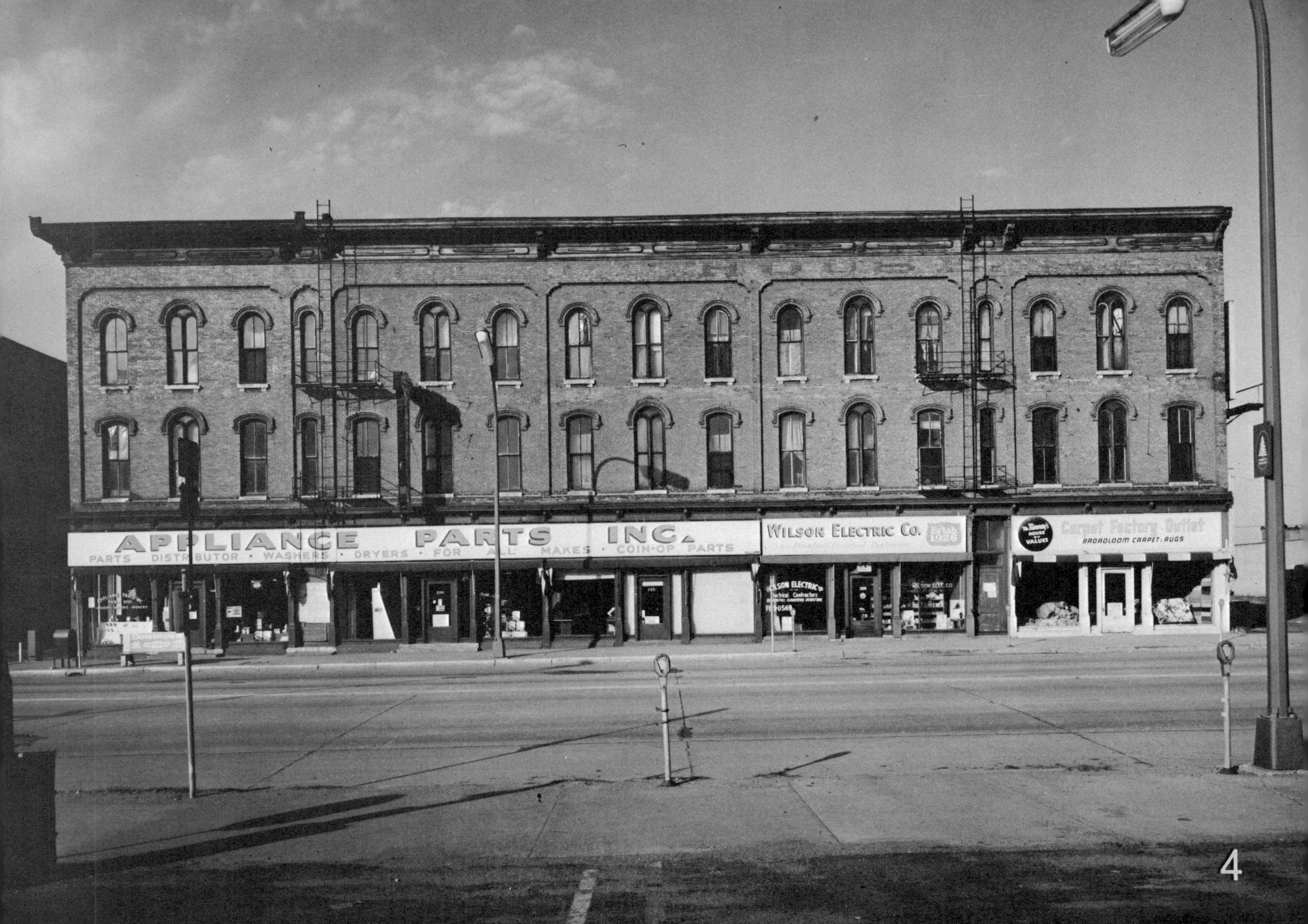
APPLIANCE PARTS INC.
PARTS DISTRIBUTOR · WASHERS · DRYERS · FOR ALL MAKES · COIN-OP PARTS
Wilson Electric Co.
Carpet Factory Outlet
BROADLOOM CARPET · RUGS
HOUSE OF VALUES
4

Pillsbury "A" Mill and Elevator   1881

Main Street Southeast

by L.S. Buffington (Minneapolis)

An extensive flour milling complex (including the Washburn mills) which developed on the west bank after 1865, suffered major destruction in the explosion and fire of May, 1878 and was rebuilt in enlarged form. But it was with the construction and milling capacity of Pillsbury "A" in 1881-82 that Minneapolis became primary flour milling center of the world, a position it maintained until after World War I.

Although alterations and structural changes have been necessary, Pillsbury "A" is fundamentally unchanged in appearance. The rock-faced limestone Buffington used tends to conceal historic precedents that enter into his designs as does the curved, slightly concave, principal facade, possibly useful but certainly not necessary for structural reasons. The divisioning and placement of the arched windows and window groups reflects but does not copy the way in which later eighteenth century English designers made use of motifs based on Roman precedent.

Quite aside from questions of architectural merit, if any one building now extant may be said to be at the center of the city's history it is Pillsbury "A". Linked as it is to a time, an industry and a prominent family, all with important roles in that history, every consideration should be given to preservation of the building if it ceases to serve as a mill.

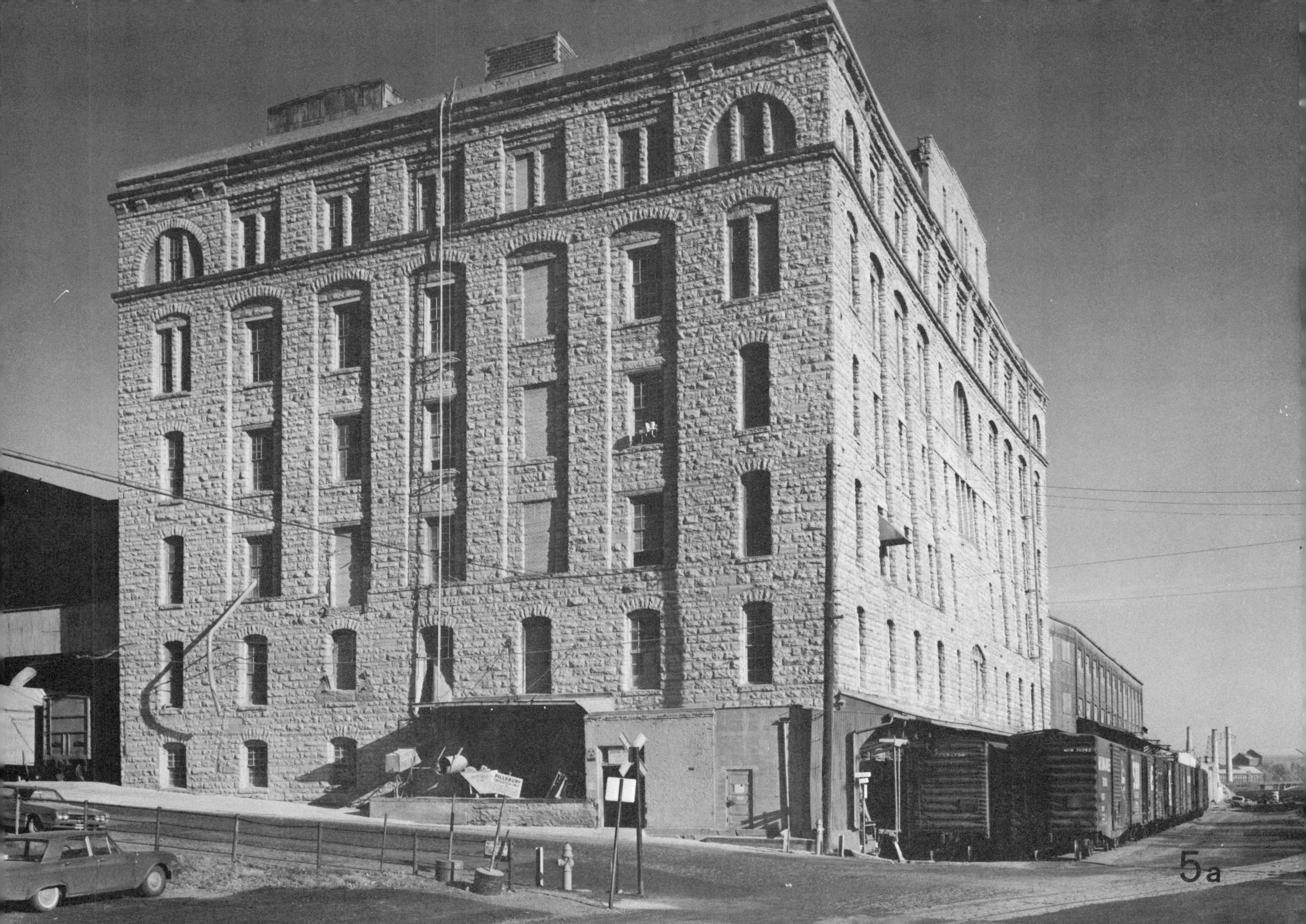
5a

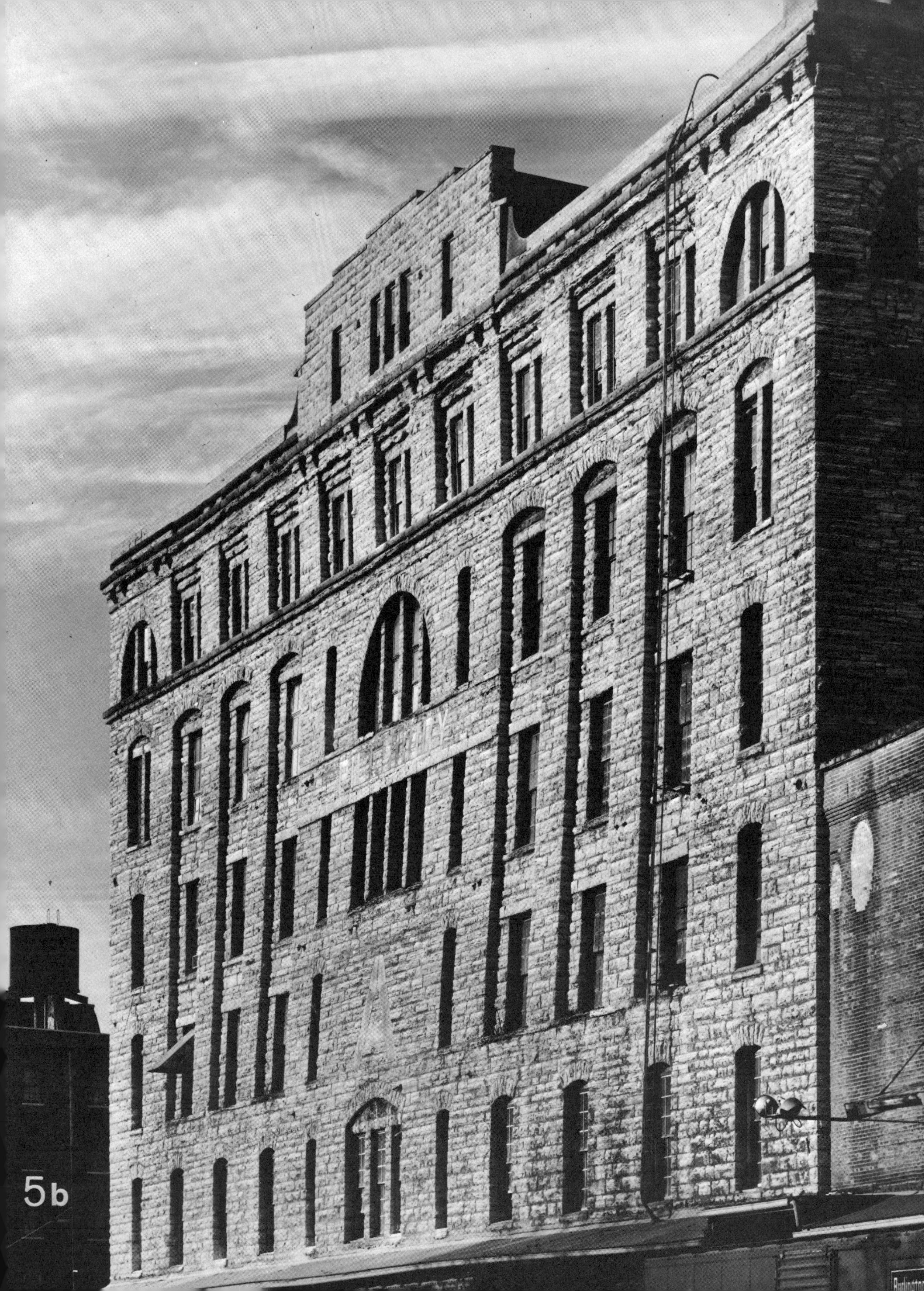
5b

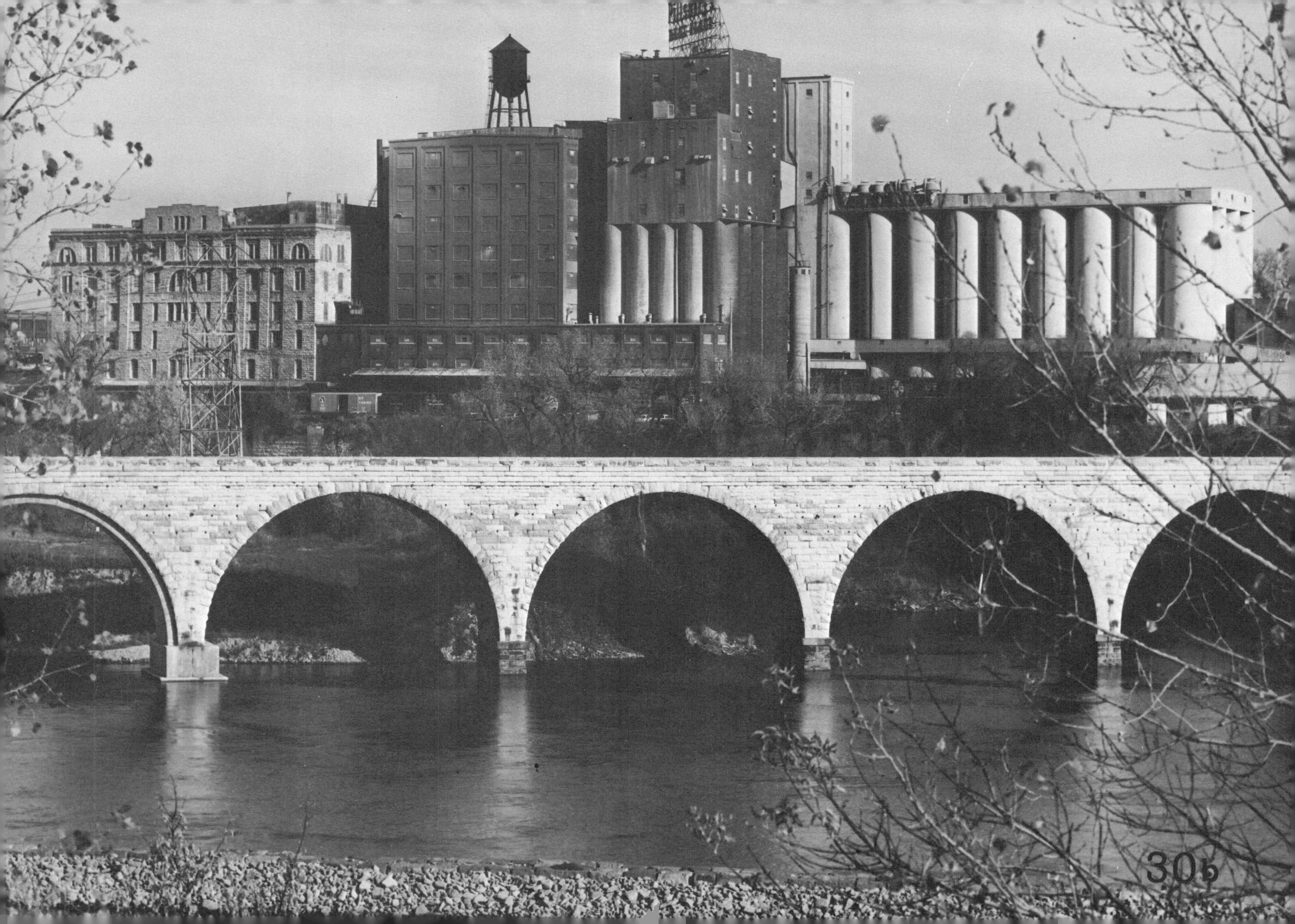

F.C. Hayer Co.   1886

(long known as National Biscuit Building)

Third Avenue North at 3rd Street

by Joseph Haley (Minneapolis)

In this six-story building with rock-faced limestone principal facades, no applied decoration is used. Aside from the simple box cornice (replacement) the effect of the building derives almost entirely from the size, placement and relationship of the multi-paned windows, which are unusually simple in form and rhythmically varied in size for that period of building. Sills and lintels are rather casually enhanced by a loosely geometric patterning of stone chisel marks, but the effectiveness of the whole design is the result of the way in which the windows are related through the continuation of sills and lintels as belting courses that define the storiation. The design quality, as in good later buildings, results from sensitivity in the handling of the structurally necessary.

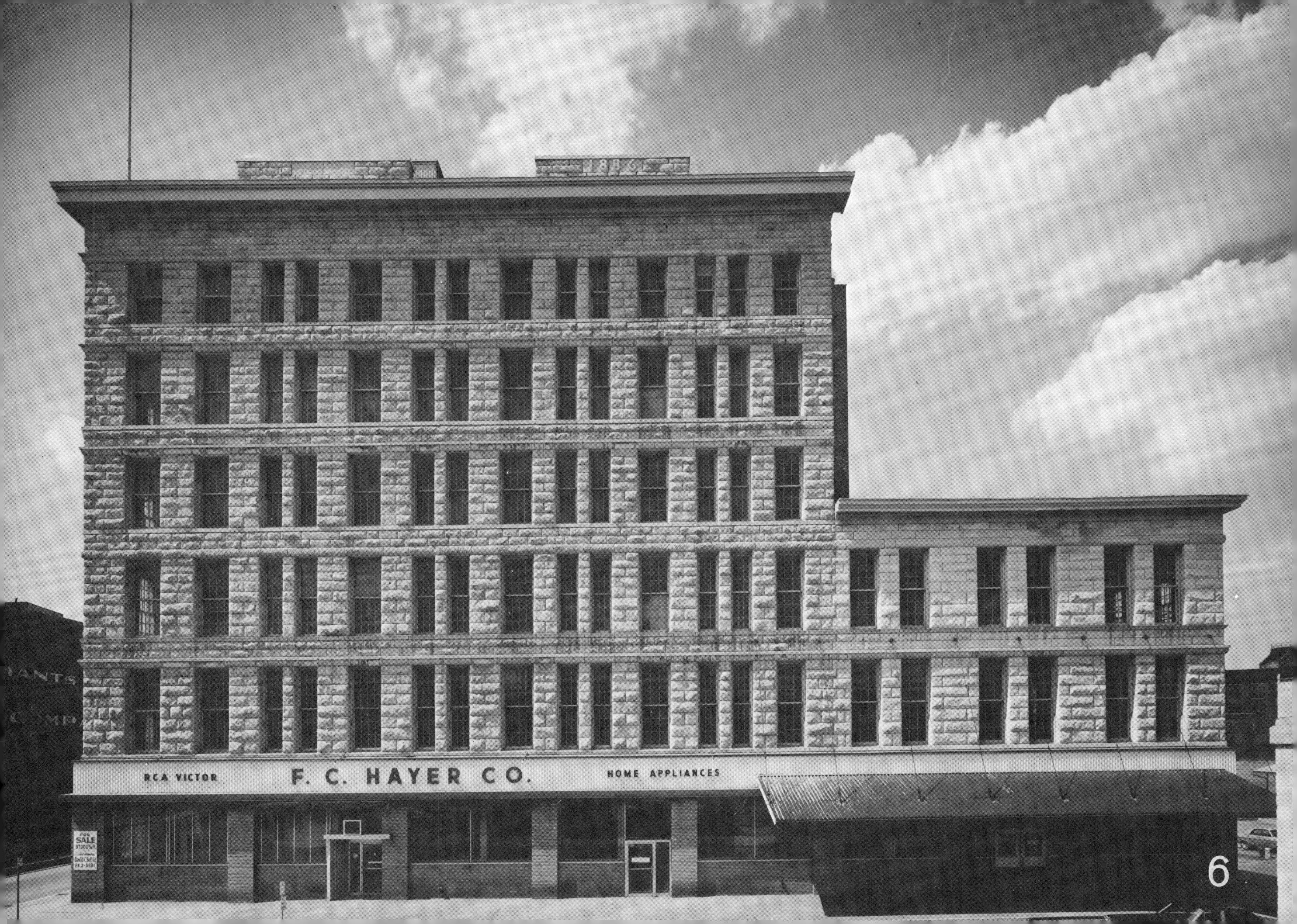

RCA VICTOR
F. C. HAYER CO.
HOME APPLIANCES

St. Joseph's (German) Roman Catholic Church   1885-86

Fourth Street North at Twelfth Avenue North

Carl Struck (Minneapolis)

Only a few of the many churches built in the Central Community
during the nineteenth century are extant today. Among those few,
St. Joseph's is unique in format in that it has an extremely broad
nave, carries twin towers with octagonal spires (destroyed by wind--
summer 1967) and makes use of detail derived from German Romanesque
prototypes, but no part of the design is copied from a known monument. The walls are of beige local brick trimmed with brown-red
sandstone. The principal facade is marked by a wheel window, by
grouped round-headed windows and by four entrances, one in each of
the square towers and two closely spaced at center front. Like the
best of the Richardson--inspired designs, St. Joseph's is less
spindly and more dignified than is the average church of the
period. Here, as in the Carpenter-Gothic churches from the mid-
century, there is an innocence or naivete about the source materials
used by the designer that we now find preferable to the hard, dead,
superficial "correctness" of most churches built in the early
twentieth century.

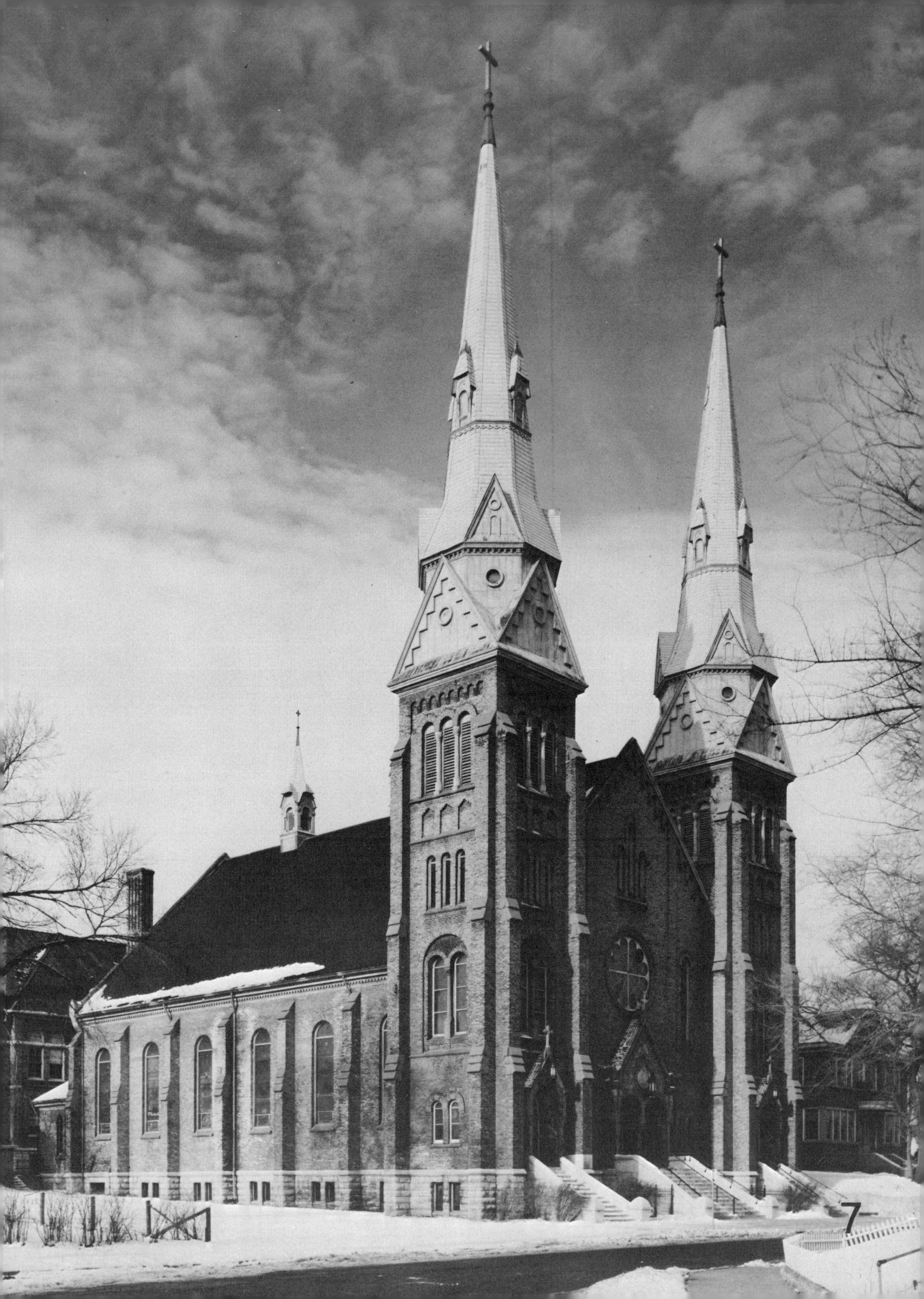

First Congregational Church   1886
Eighth Avenue and Fifth Street Southeast
by W.H. Hayes (Minneapolis)

In the combination of rock-faced dark red sandstone, a major entrance tower with a tall spire (destroyed by wind--summer 1967) based on English 'Victorian Gothic' prototypes and very large, round-arch windows of the type popularized by H.H. Richardson, First Congregational is typical for its period, but better than the average design of the type.

It is an "Akron Plan" church, much admired during the later decades of the nineteenth century. The name stems from the fact that the plan was first used in a Methodist church at Akron, Ohio in 1868. The plan was devised in response to the bishop's demand for a plan that was flexible enough to allow for a "togetherness" of all who attended Sunday School and Church but also allowed, easily and quickly, for a "separateness" when the congregation would be separated into groups on the basis of age and sex for purposes of religious instruction adapted to the various levels of maturity. The church auditorium proper could be linked to the adjoining Sunday School by large counter-balanced doors or panels that slid into floor slots for the togetherness. The Sunday School quarters consisted of a large central space round which the classrooms, often in two tiers, opened to the central area by means of a folding wall or doors. Many Akron Plan churches contained kitchens, made provision for the serving of banquet suppers and provided other "club" facilities. In these several matters, the church plan is closely linked to the educational aspects of the Chatauqua Movement and it recognized and fostered the emergence of the protestant church as a type of social center rather than as a sanctuary in the strict sense.

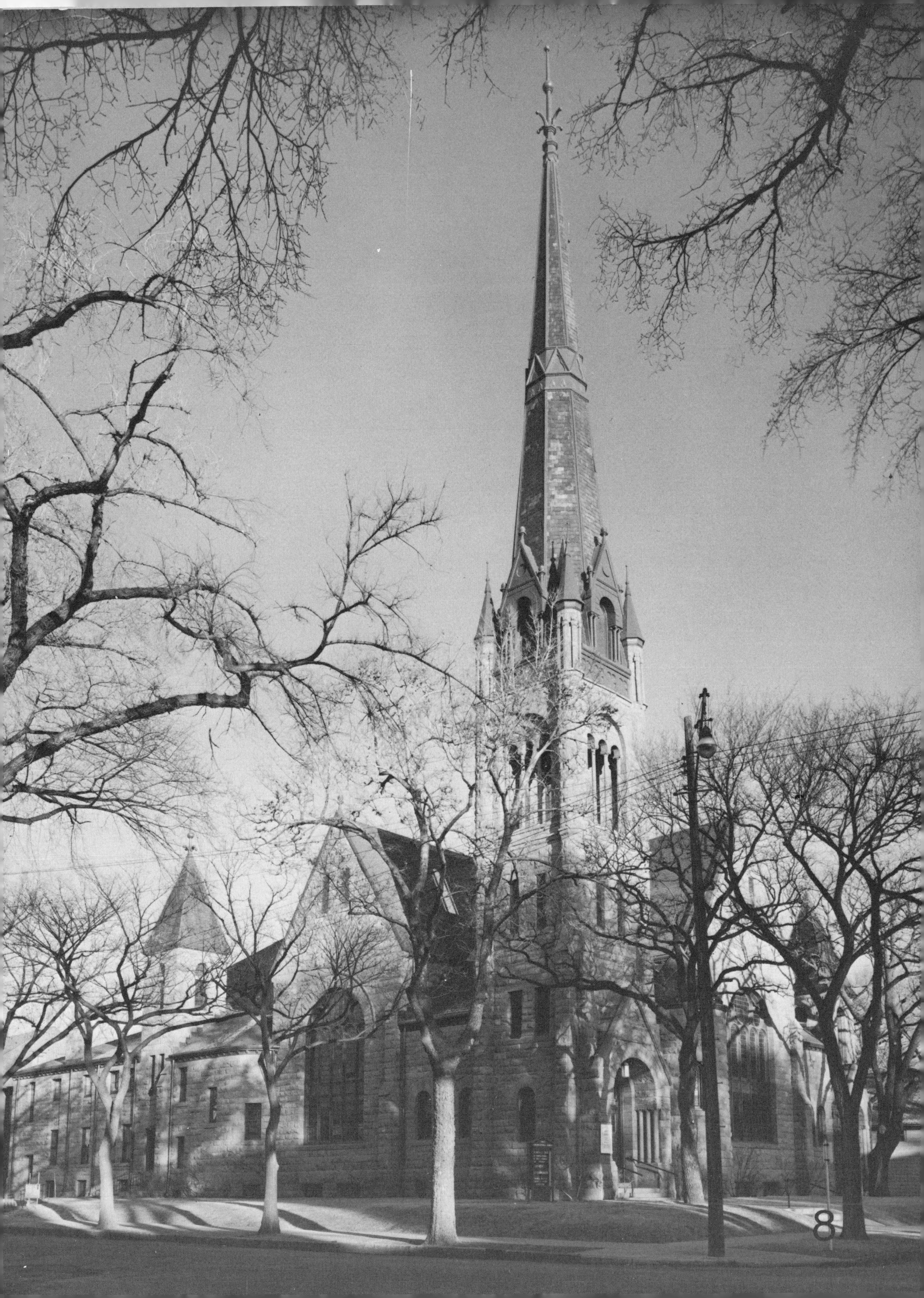

Pillsbury Hall   1887-88

Pillsbury Drive - University of Minnesota

by L.S. Buffington (Minneapolis) (Harvey Ellis designer)

In the course of the 1880's many so-called Richardsonian
Romanesque buildings were erected in Minneapolis, but very few
have survived. Although this building gives ample evidence of
its designer's debt to no less than seven designs from the
H.H. Richardson office and one from that of McKim, Mead and
White, Pillsbury Hall nevertheless is one of the few campus
structures that is impressive in its massiveness and distinctive
in character.

Linked as it is to an important formative period of University
history, it has value over and beyond the strengths or weaknesses
of its design. Its future deserves the most careful consideration.

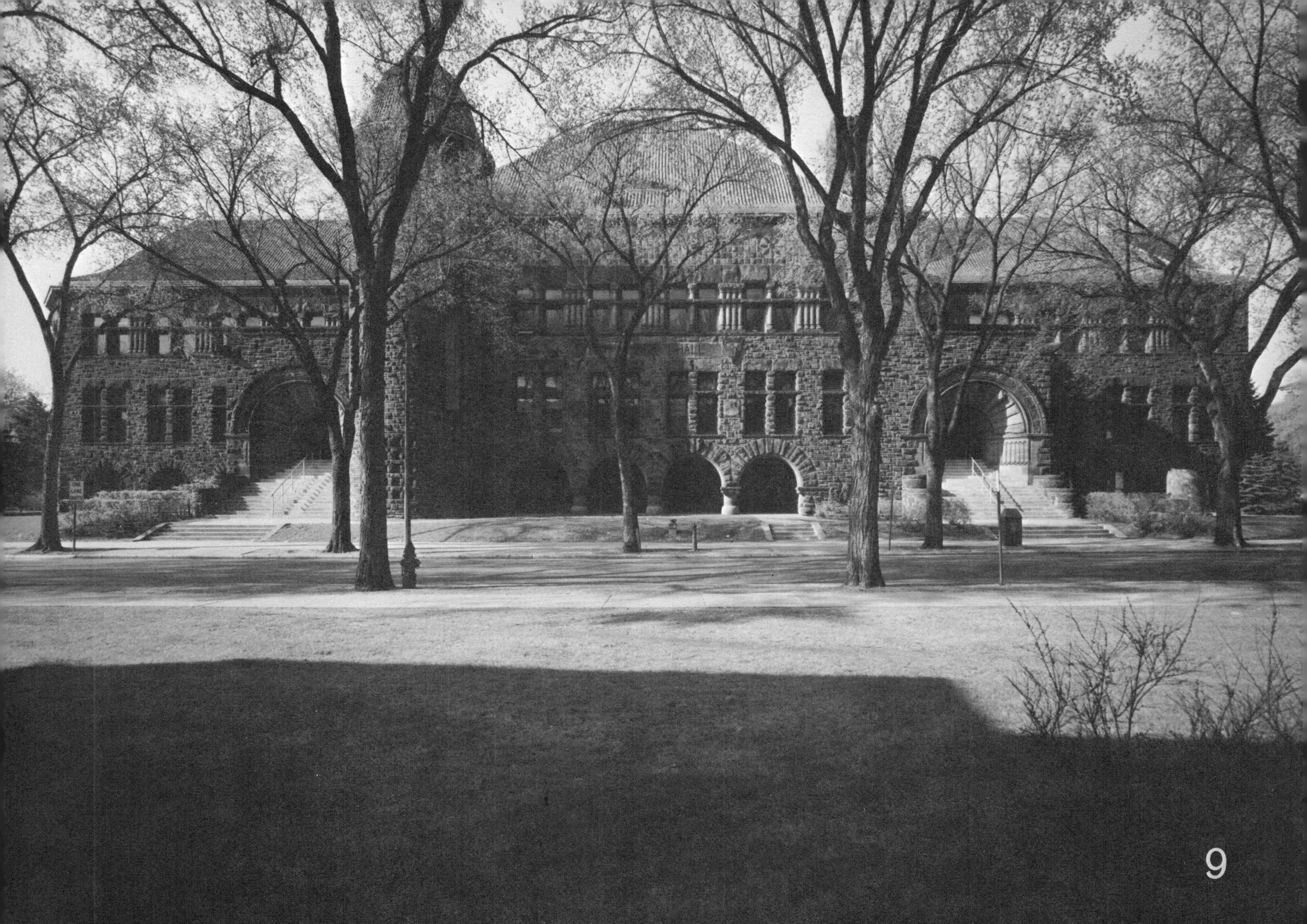
HALL

The City Hall-County Courthouse   1889-1905

Fourth to Fifth Streets - Third to Fourth Avenue South

by Long and Kees (Minneapolis)

The sources for the design of the Ortonville Granite City-
County building are in the Allegheny County Buildings at Pittsburgh
(1883-87) by H.H. Richardson of Boston. The Long and Kees design
is typically "Western" for its period in that it is more complex in
its composition, less unified in the relation among its parts, and
structurally more open--particularly in the very open basement
story---than is Richardson's parent building. Despite such faults,
and a lessened degree of subtlety than Richardson realized in his
designs, this is a building of power and dignity which has for a
long time not been properly appreciated.

The copper roof which replaces the more heavily textured
original, lacks the sense of substantiality demanded by the rock-
faced masonry walls below it. Extensive and inept interior alterations in recent years have in every case violated the spirit
and the quality of the original design. From a distance the
building is a major landmark in the central area skyline, but it
would be much enhanced by an adequate site--from opening of ample
areas on both the Fourth and Fifth Street facades--so the design
could be properly seen from the immediately surrounding areas.

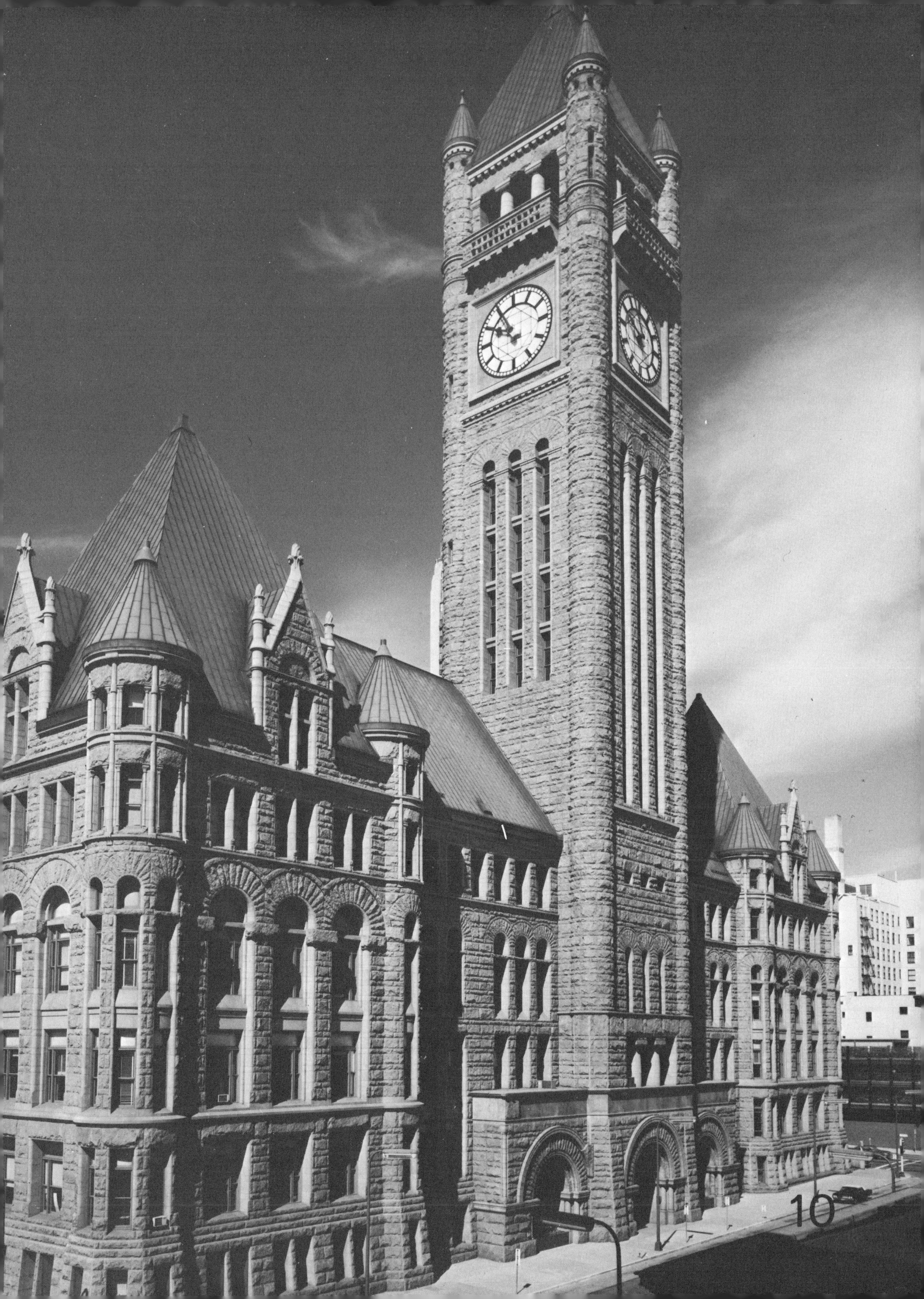

10

The Flour Exchange   1892/1909

310 Fourth Avenue South

by Long and Kees (Minneapolis)

Completed through four stories at the time of the financial
crisis in 1893, construction was stopped until 1909 when the
seven upper stories were added according to the original design.
In the elimination of applied ornament, except for minor detail at
the entrance arch and on the soffit of the simple cornice (removed),
the Flour Exchange marks a complete break with the modes of architectural design then practiced in this city. The clarity and
simplicity of the design are largely due to the use of an unbroken
sweep from battered basement story to cornice, and from the use of
spandrels recessed between the piers. In these features there is
debt to both Holabird and Roche and to Sullivan. Recently the
brick masonry has most unfortunately been painted a bald and
glaring white which destroys the dark-light balance established in
the original design.

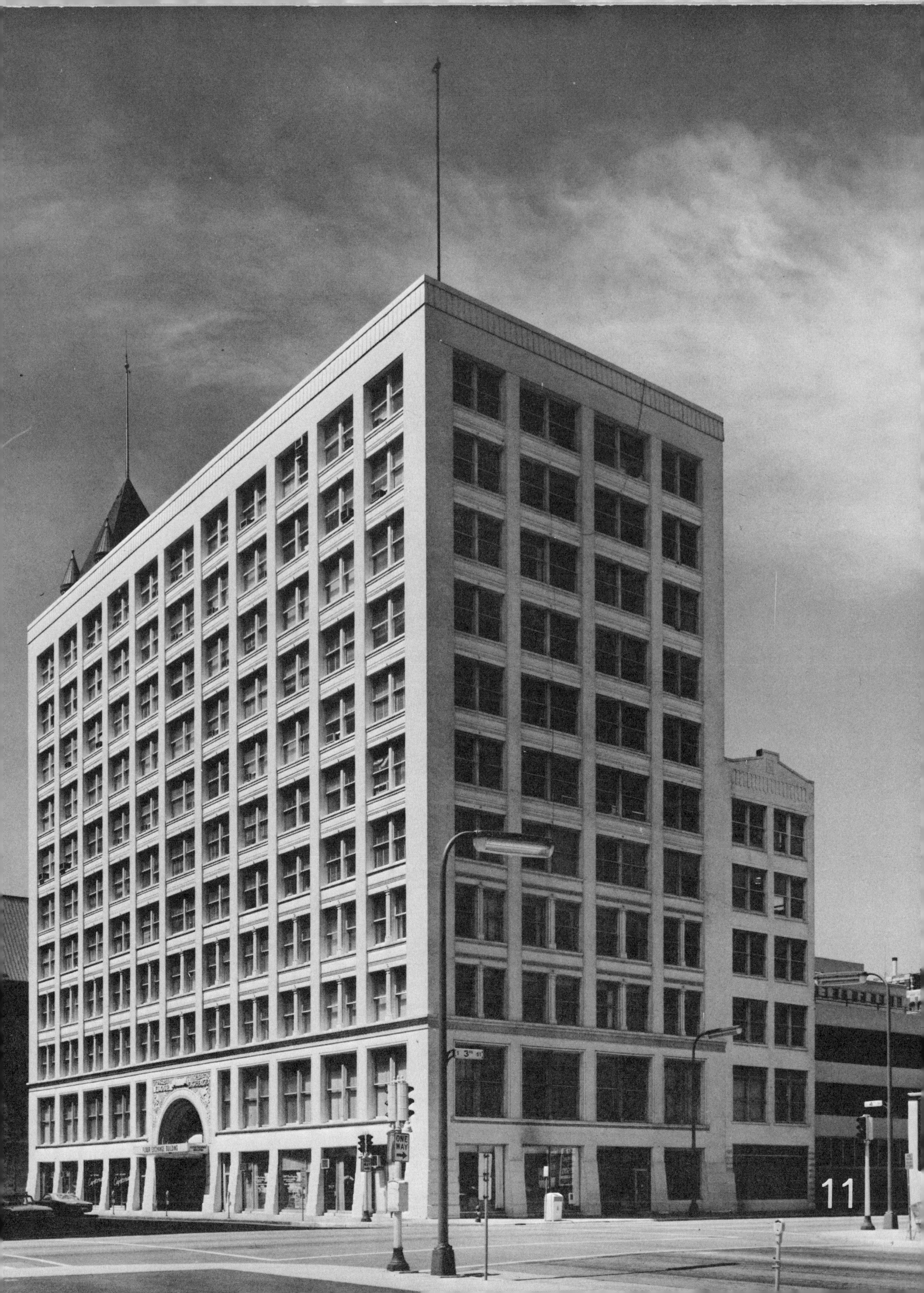
FLOUR EXCHANGE
FLOUR EXCHANGE BUILDING
3RD ST
ONE WAY

The Grain Exchange   1900--1902

(Originally Chamber of Commerce)

Fourth Avenue South at Fourth St.

by Kees and Colburn (Minneapolis)

The ten story Grain Exchange was one of the two buildings in Minneapolis first to make use of a steel frame. In general format and organization, in slab cornice (removed), in recessed spandrels, and in an elaborate terra-cotta ornament of flat, geometrically based tracery, the Grain Exchange derives from Louis Sullivan's Wainwright Building at St. Louis of 1890-91. While the Minneapolis design gives the effect of being less assured in the proportioning of its elements and is visually less strong than the parent work-- primarily because of the windows introduced near the corners of the composition--it is still a handsome and dignified structure, far superior in quality of design to most of the Minneapolis office buildings erected in the half-century after 1900.

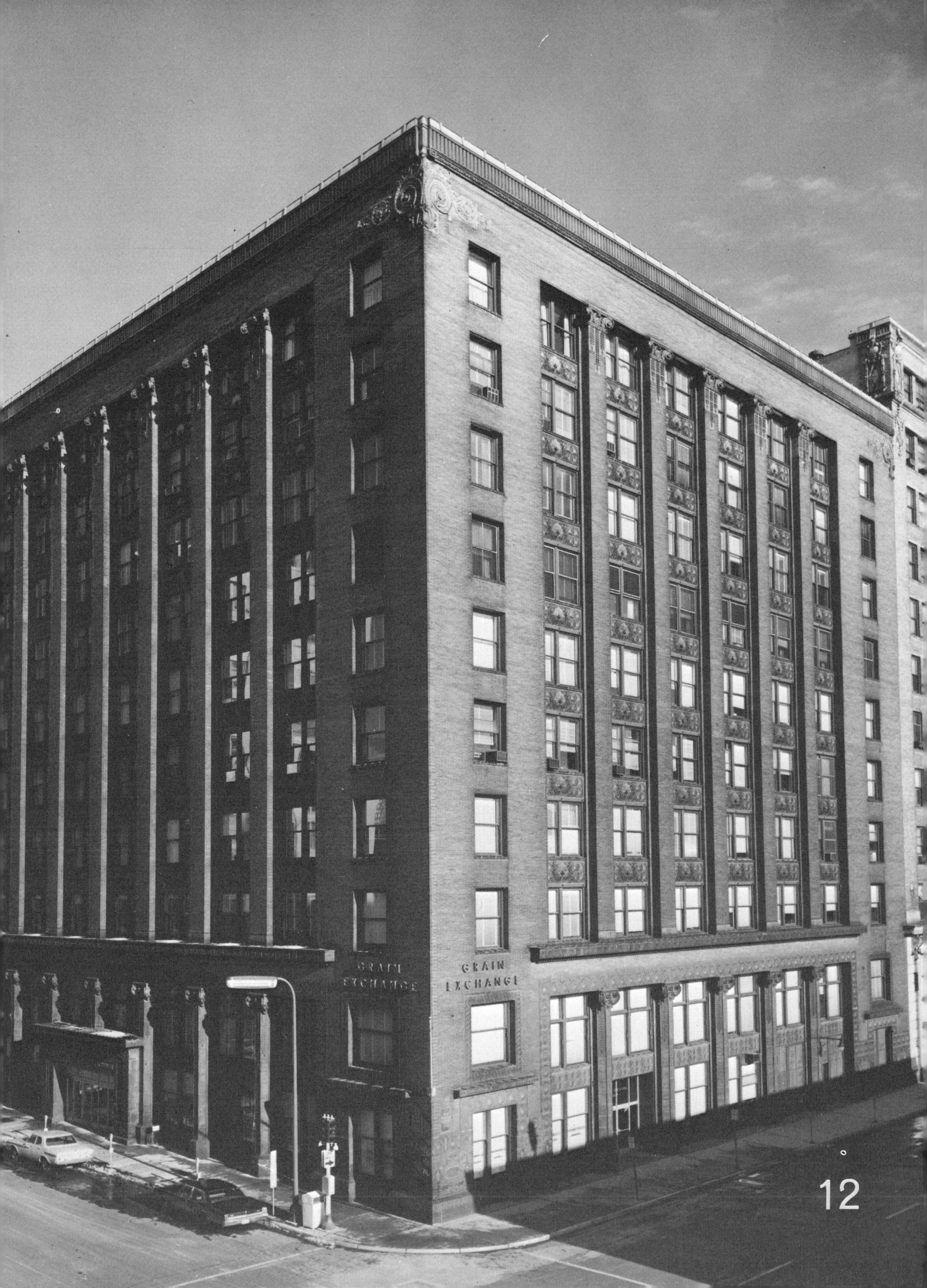
GRAIN
EXCHANGE
GRAIN
EXCHANGE

Advance Thresher Building   1900

   <u>and</u>

Emerson-Newton Plow Co.   1904

700 and 704 South Third Street

by Kees and Colburn (Minneapolis)

These two manufacturing-assembly plants for farm machinery are almost unique among Minneapolis buildings on adjoining lots, in that the architects (the same in each case) recognized the architectural character of the earlier building in designing that erected later. Further, they skillfully diverted attention from the fact that the two structures, while equal in height, do not have the same number of stories. In the massing of openings, use of a slab cornice and of orange brick, the designs are distinctly reminiscent of Louis Sullivan. The terra cotta ornament however, weakly Neo-Classic, is unfortunately out of character with other elements of the design. Together with the Pittsburgh Plate Glass building at 616 South Third Street, they constitute the best designed industrial group of buildings in the central community.

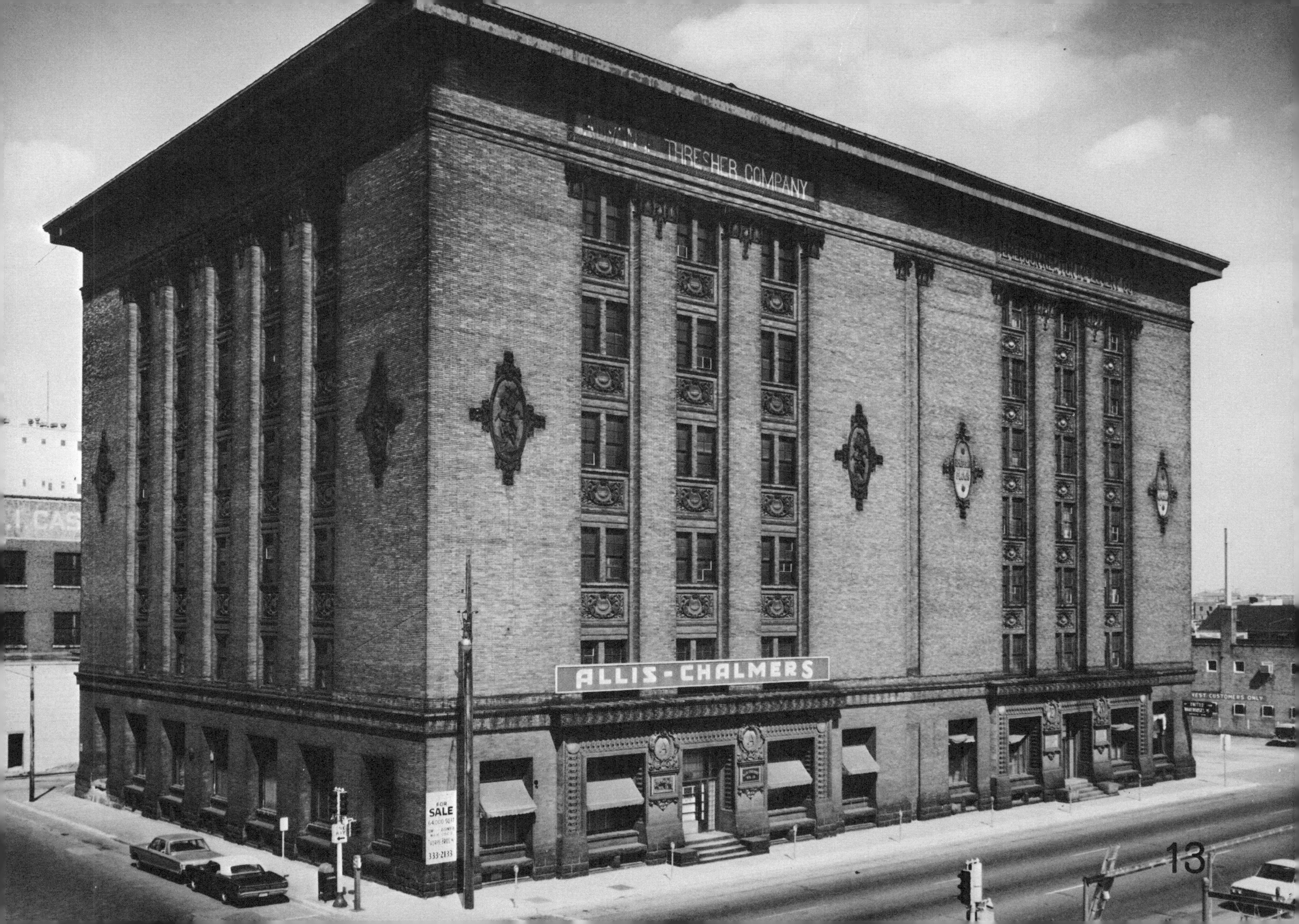
THRESHER COMPANY
ALLIS-CHALMERS
FOR SALE
333-2133
BEST CUSTOMERS ONLY

Deere and Weber Co.   1902

(now Midwest Merchandise Building)

800-818 Washington Avenue North

by Kees and Colburn (Minneapolis)

In this six-story building of beige brick, Kees and Colburn
stripped away virtually all ornament. The architectural effect,
which arises out of the scale of the structure and the proportioning
of its parts, is intensified by the directness with which the form
is developed: a heavy wall, battered in the basement story, rises
uninterruptedly to an outward curving parapet that terminates the
composition. Deep window reveals, defined with sharp precision,
accentuate the weight and solidity of the walls.

The use of a range of arched openings that link the windows
of several stories in one cohesive design motif probably had its
source in the work of H.H. Richardson, as the flaring parapet
probably was based on the Burnham and Root design for the
Monadnock Building at Chicago of 1889-91---but, the Deere and Weber
building goes beyond derivation and is a fine design in its own
very carefully controlled terms. We know of no other structure in
Minneapolis in which mortar joints here laid flush in a mortar
slightly darker than the brick, have been used with a sensitivity
and precision that both enriches the surface and intensifies its
sense of weighty solidity and permanence. Neither the remodeled
entry nor the glass brick used to fill in the great, segmentally-
arched windows of the third story are worthy of the building.

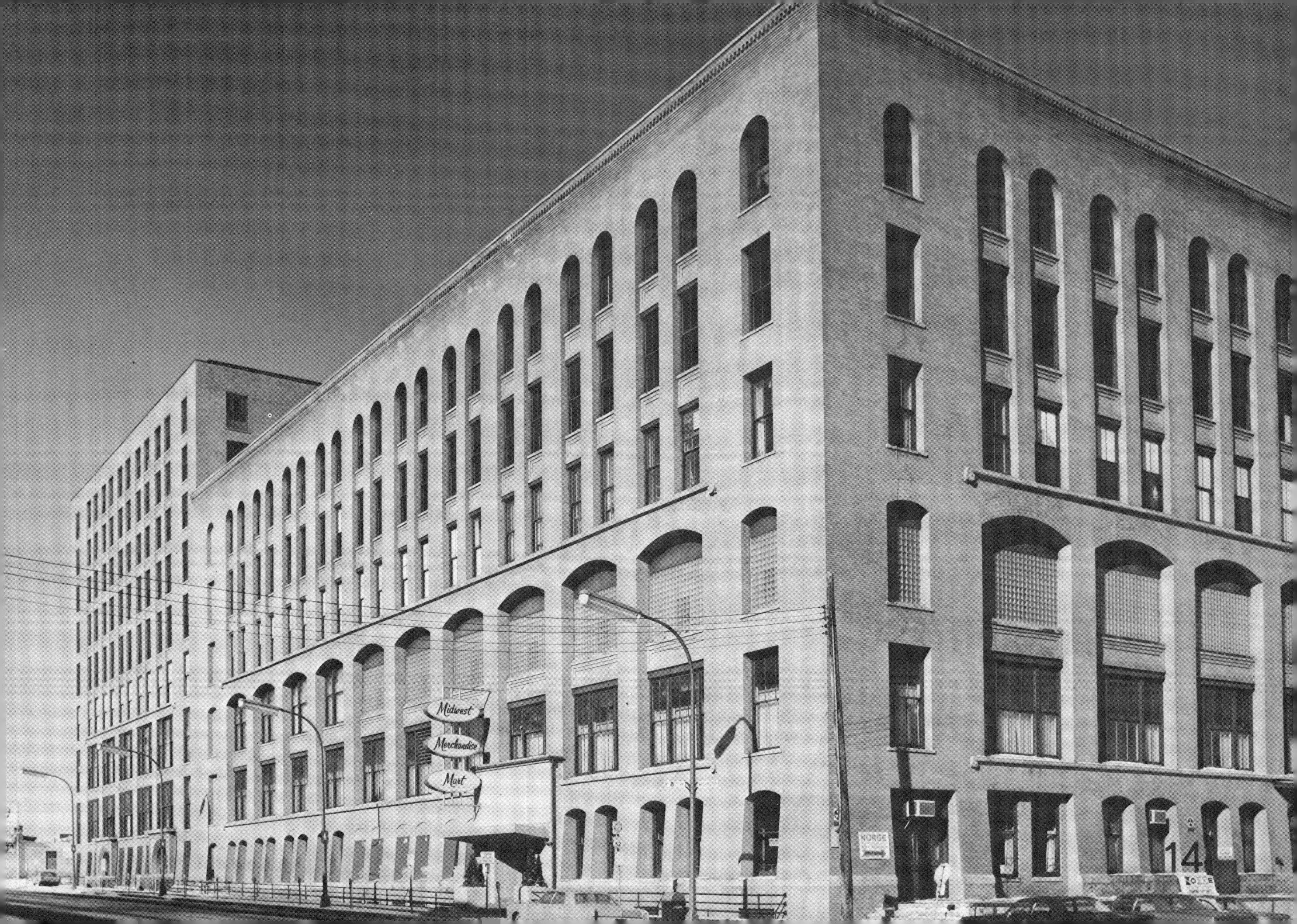

Midwest
Merchandise
Mart
NORGE
14

Swan Turnblad residence   1903

(American Swedish Institute)

2600 Park Avenue

by Boehme and Cordella (Minneapolis)

Although extravagantly picturesque houses have been widely
admired from time to time, they have appealed to relatively few
of the Minneapolitans who were in a position to indulge a taste
for the exotic. Among such houses built in the city, the former
Turnblad mansion is one of few to survive. Here, as in many
buildings of the general type, dramatic effects are gained by
means of arbitrary asymmetry and through irregularities in plan
that serve no purpose other than to mask the basically simple
mass of the structure.

The house is of interest primarily as evidence of romantic
spirit expressed to the point of folly, which recurs so per-
sistently in American architecture that it cannot be denied a
place in our social and cultural history.

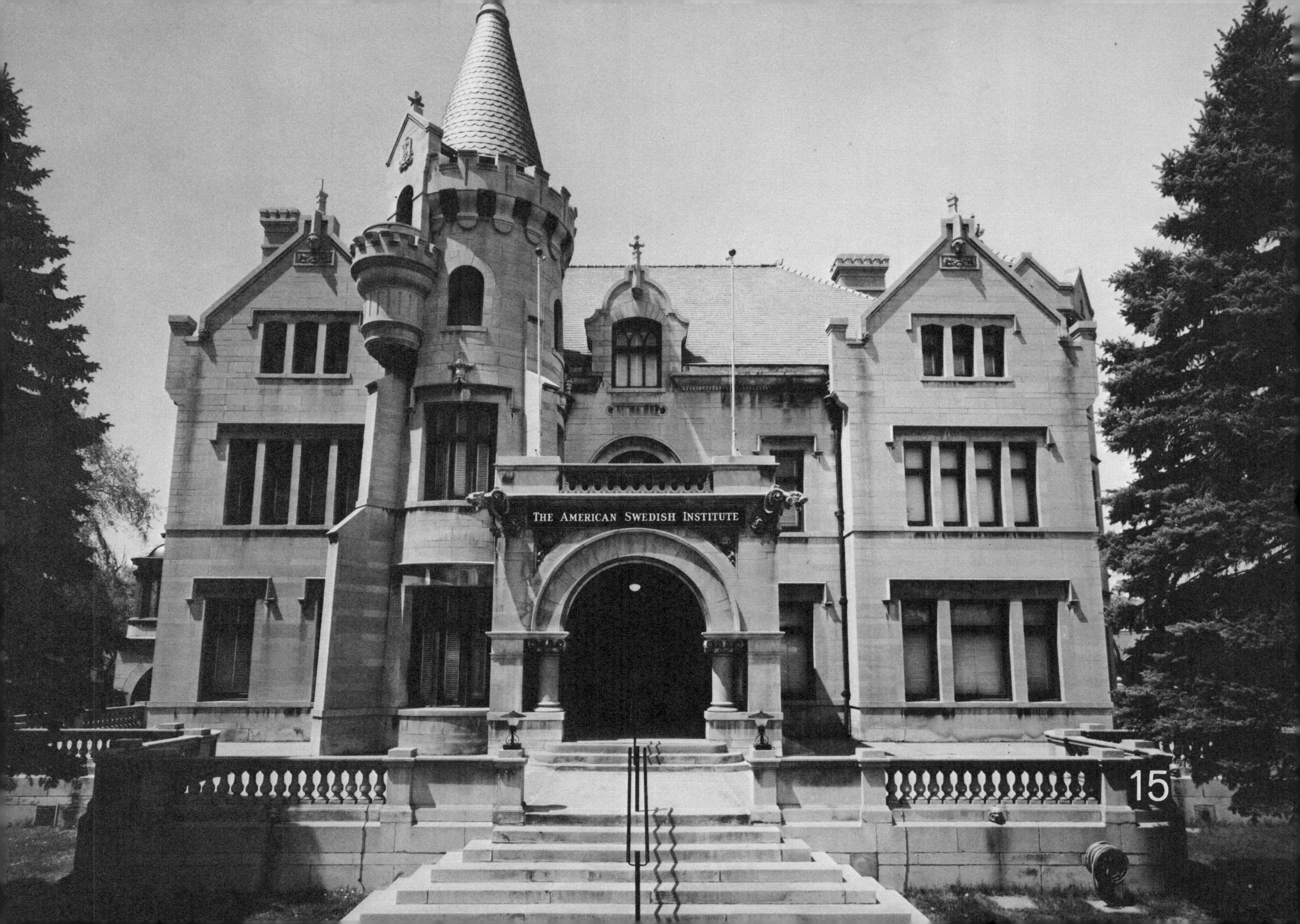

15

Butler Brothers   1906-1908

(now vacated)

First Avenue North at 6th Street

by Harry Jones (Minneapolis)

Here again recessed spandrels are the means through which the many openings of several stories are linked into an "arcade" form that unifies the elements of the facade into a cohesive design.

Jones used a deep wine-red brick, semi-glazed in the basement story and parapet, for this sombre and elegant wholesale warehouse and office building. The design is not lacking in reference to both its immediate past and to the late middle ages. The arch forms, pointed and segmental, the corbeled parapets and the severity of the massive walls are somewhat reminiscent of Gothic Communal palaces in the hill towns of Tuscany and of the Palace of the Popes at Avignon, but the inspiration for the design well might have been Sullivan's Chicago Cold Storage Warehouse of 1891.

Notation of possible sources and influences that may have influenced Jones is made solely for the purpose of linking the design to modes that were then current, not in a negatively critical spirit. Butler Brothers is of conventional (masonry-timber), heavy, mill-construction, not of a modern, framed construction. It is a design on which most architects and any city could look with pride and pleasure. Now vacant, its conservation and preservation deserve the most careful consideration.

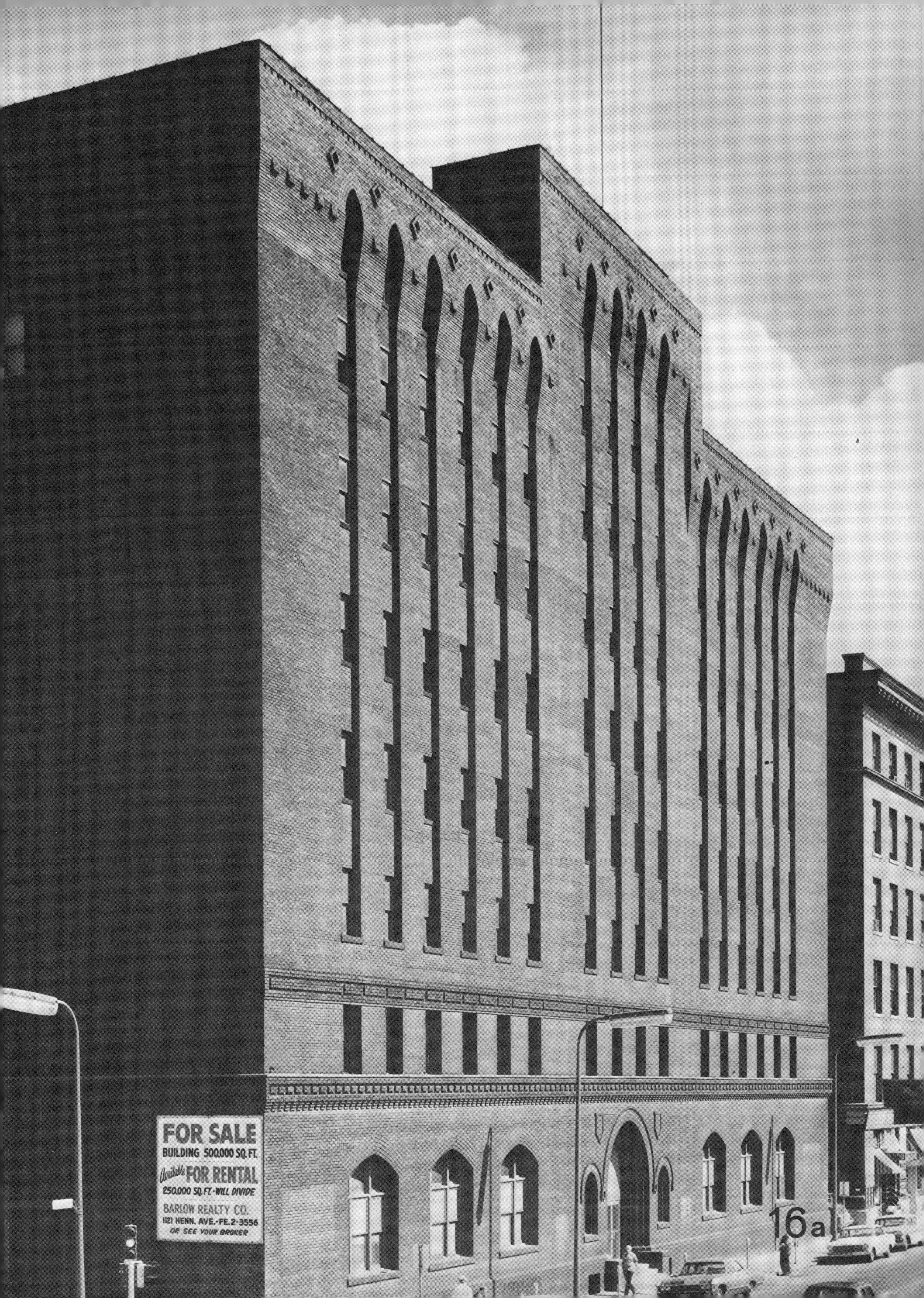

FOR SALE
BUILDING 500,000 SQ. FT.
Available FOR RENTAL
250,000 SQ. FT.-WILL DIVIDE
BARLOW REALTY CO.
1121 HENN. AVE.-FE.2-3556
OR SEE YOUR BROKER

16a

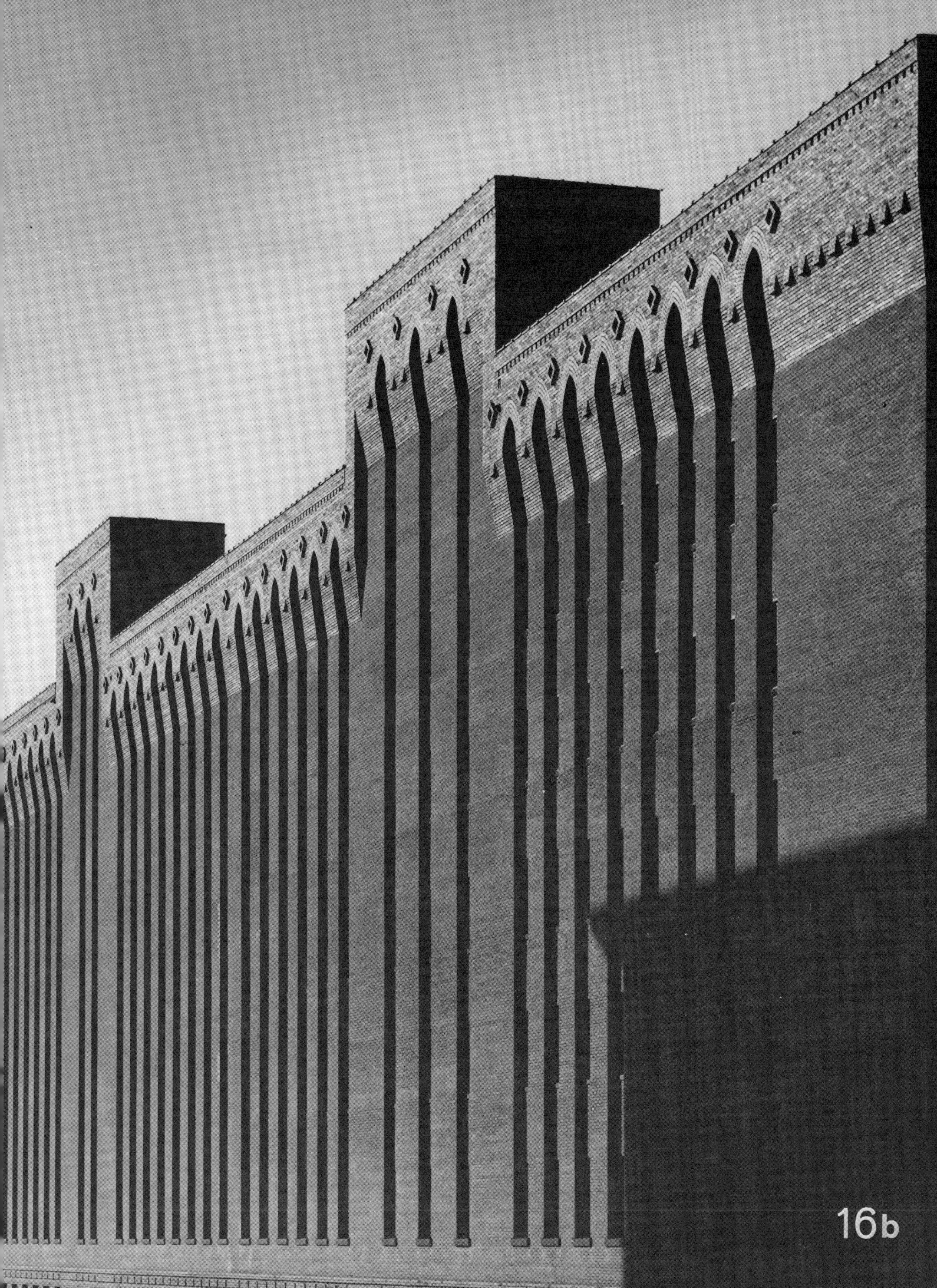
16b

Plymouth Congregational Church   1907-08

1900 Nicollet Avenue

Shepley-Rutan-Coolidge (Boston)

For the majority of Gothic-revival churches the design source--
however remote---had been the cathedral, scaled down sometimes to toy
size. Here the Boston architects (successors to Richardson) ob-
tained a less pretentious appearance--however derivative---by using
the parish church of rural England as a source. The tower is square
and heavy, the nave broad and the eaves low. The vari-colored,
random laid, seamfaced granite walls and the heavy, hammer beam
trusses are departures from the design norms favored at the time.
The comparative informality of the materials and massing of building
elements make it seem more appropriate to the casually developed
area than would a more formal design. Necessary additions to the
church complex have been consistent with the original design but
now tend to dominate the church proper as it is seen from Nicollet
Avenue.

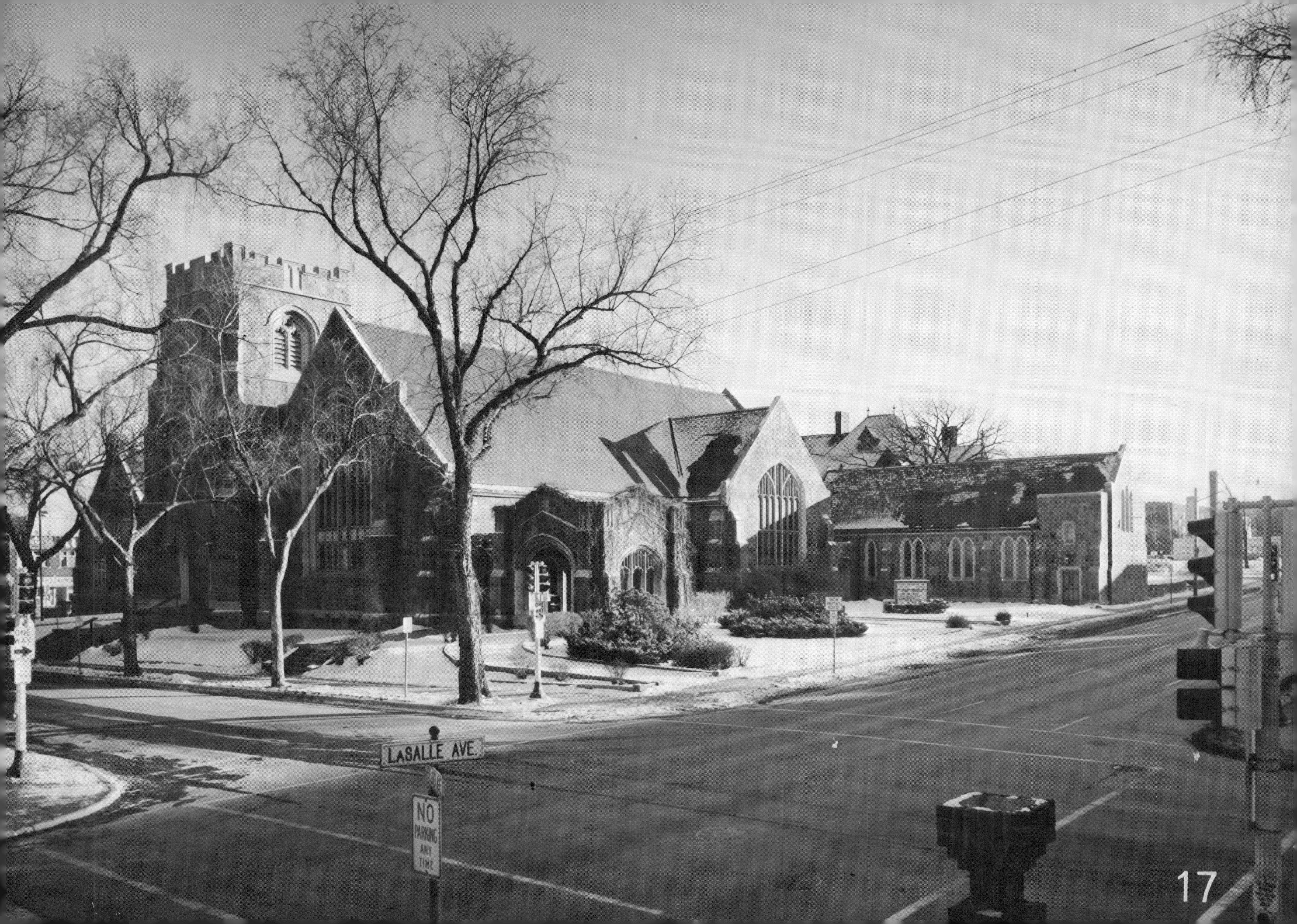
ONE WAY
LASALLE AVE.
NO PARKING ANY TIME

Cathedral Church of St. Mark (Episcopal)   1908

519 Oak Grove (at Lyndale)

by E.H. Hewitt (Minneapolis)

  and

Hennepin Avenue Methodist Church   1914

511 Groveland (at Lyndale)

by Hewitt and Brown (Minneapolis)

American architects generally have given little attention to an exacting, archeological correctness in making their borrowings from the styles of earlier eras. All but the exceptional architects have been content with loose approximation. In the early years of this century much talk, perhaps inspired by men like Ralph Adams Cram, was devoted to the importance of "correct" usage, but the desire to be correct was, in general, satisfied by nothing more exacting than attention to general compositional effects and to selected detail. Both St. Mark's and Hennepin Methodist were presented as Early English Gothic but the extensive schooling of their architect is reflected in their engineering rather than in the quality of their designs.

Despite the fact that the high, narrow nave of St. Mark's is somewhat dwarfed by a too large and too heavy tower and that the squatty and complicated mass of Hennepin Methodist is capped by an underscaled lantern and fleche, both structures are important elements in the area immediately south of Loring Park. Both belong to that sizable group of buildings in which community importance is determined by where the building is and by how it relates to other structures rather than by strictly architectural merit.

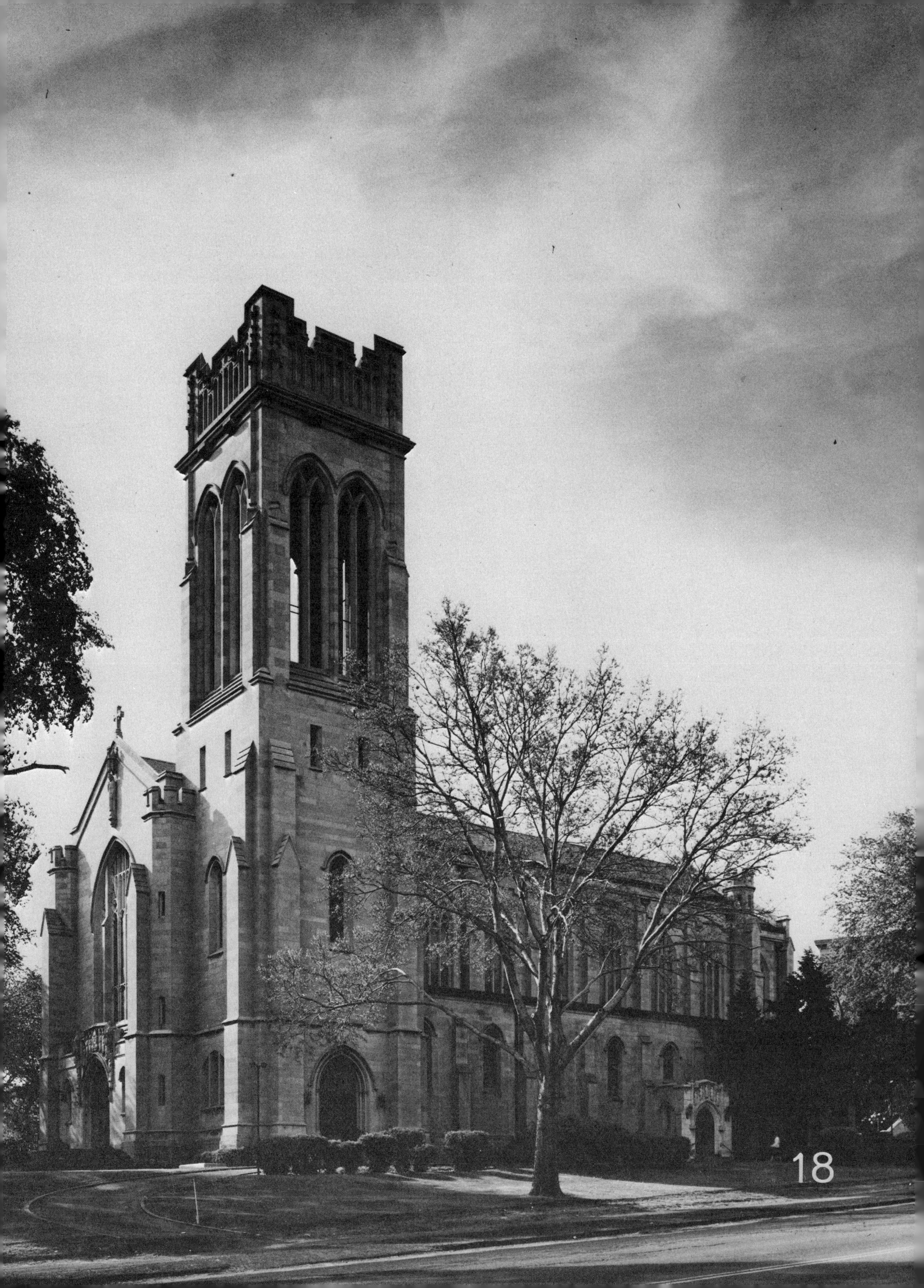

18

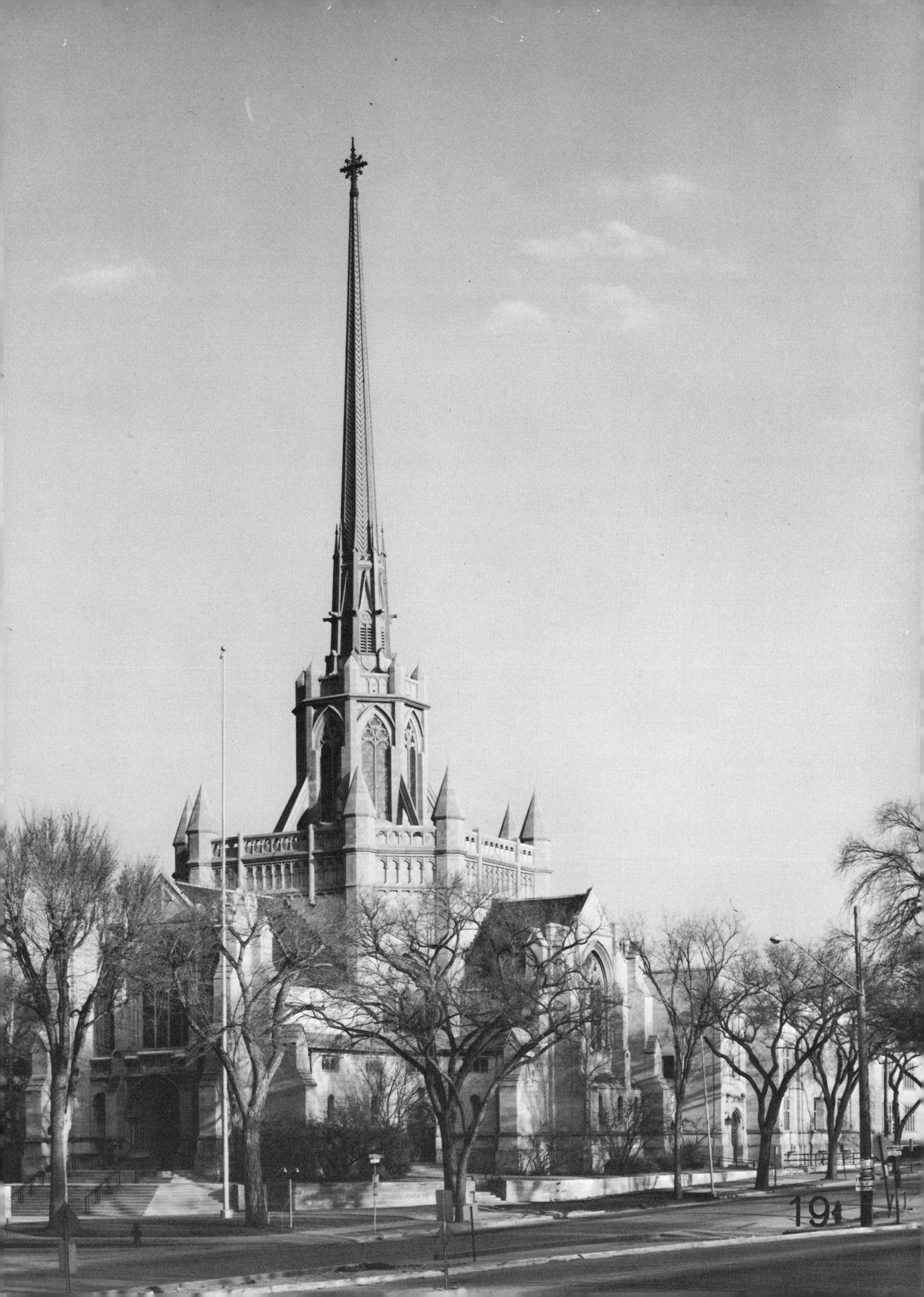

Basilica of St. Mary   1908-ca. 1925

Hennepin Avenue at 16th Street

by E. Louis Masqueray (St. Paul)

    The recurrent interest in classicized forms that continued
into the twentieth century had little effect on the design of
churches in this area. Most prominent among those that did depart
from one or another form of medievalism is the Roman Catholic
Pro-Cathedral. The stated aim of the Paris Ecole trained architect
was to develop a "Modern Renaissance" design of grandeur and
simplicity. While none of these terms would today be considered
particularly appropriate to this cumbersome, loosely Neo-Baroque
composition, the careful attention that was given to the siting
of the structure is worthy of emulation. Placed as it is, the
church is a focal point for the traffic arteries from the south
and west, defines a change in direction in a major traffic route
and helps to establish a northerly limit for the Loring Park area.

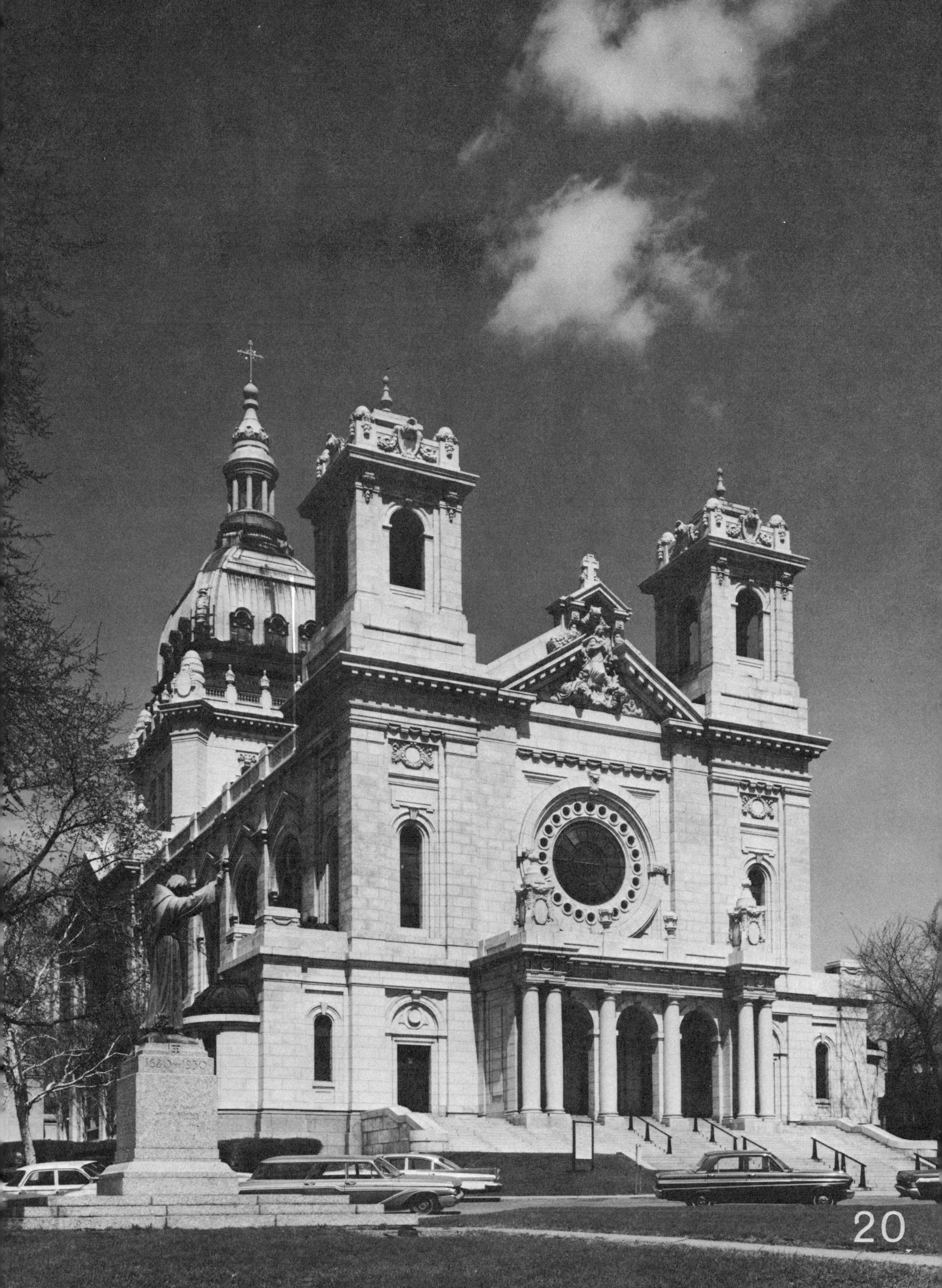

1680—1930

Alfred Pillsbury residence   1903

116 E. 22nd Street

by Ernest Kennedy (Minneapolis)

   and

Charles S. Pillsbury residence   1912

100 E. 22nd Street

by Hewitt and Brown (Minneapolis)

From the early nineties through the nineteen-twenties the so-called English Gothic style gained wide acceptance in the field of domestic architecture. "English Gothic" was loosely used to describe any feature, detail or composition that was derived from the Tudor, Jacobean or Elizabethan and realized in stone, brick, half-timber or a combination of the three. The houses range in their mode of design from severe, cold and rather bald, as seen in the residence at 2205 Park Avenue of 1902, to the overly ornamented and meaninglessly irregular, as seen in 325 Clifton Avenue of 1904. Two that fall within the general type and happily avoid both extremes are the stone houses for Alfred and Charles S. Pillsbury.

   Of rock-faced local limestone in the case of the older building and dressed limestone in the later, both houses use ornamental detail sparingly, clearly show the geometric nature of the several parts and use transoms, mullions and string courses to tie the elements into a whole that is simple, solid and dignified. It is worth noting that the good qualities of each building are fortified by reason of the fact that the structure on the adjoining property is related in scale as it is in style.   Both are presently unoccupied. Their demolition would be a misfortune

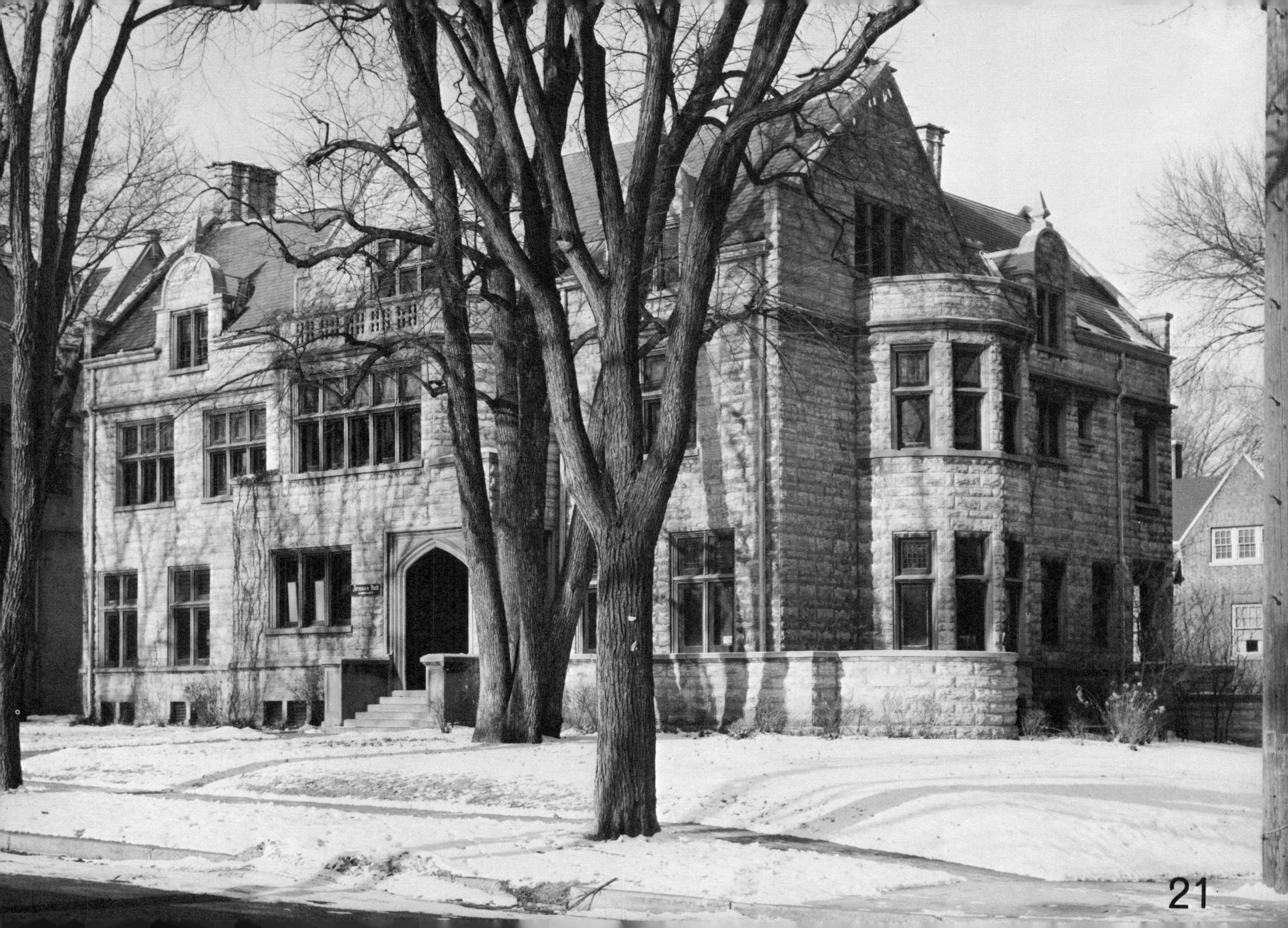

for the surrounding area, which more closely than any other in the city has the character of a cultural district.

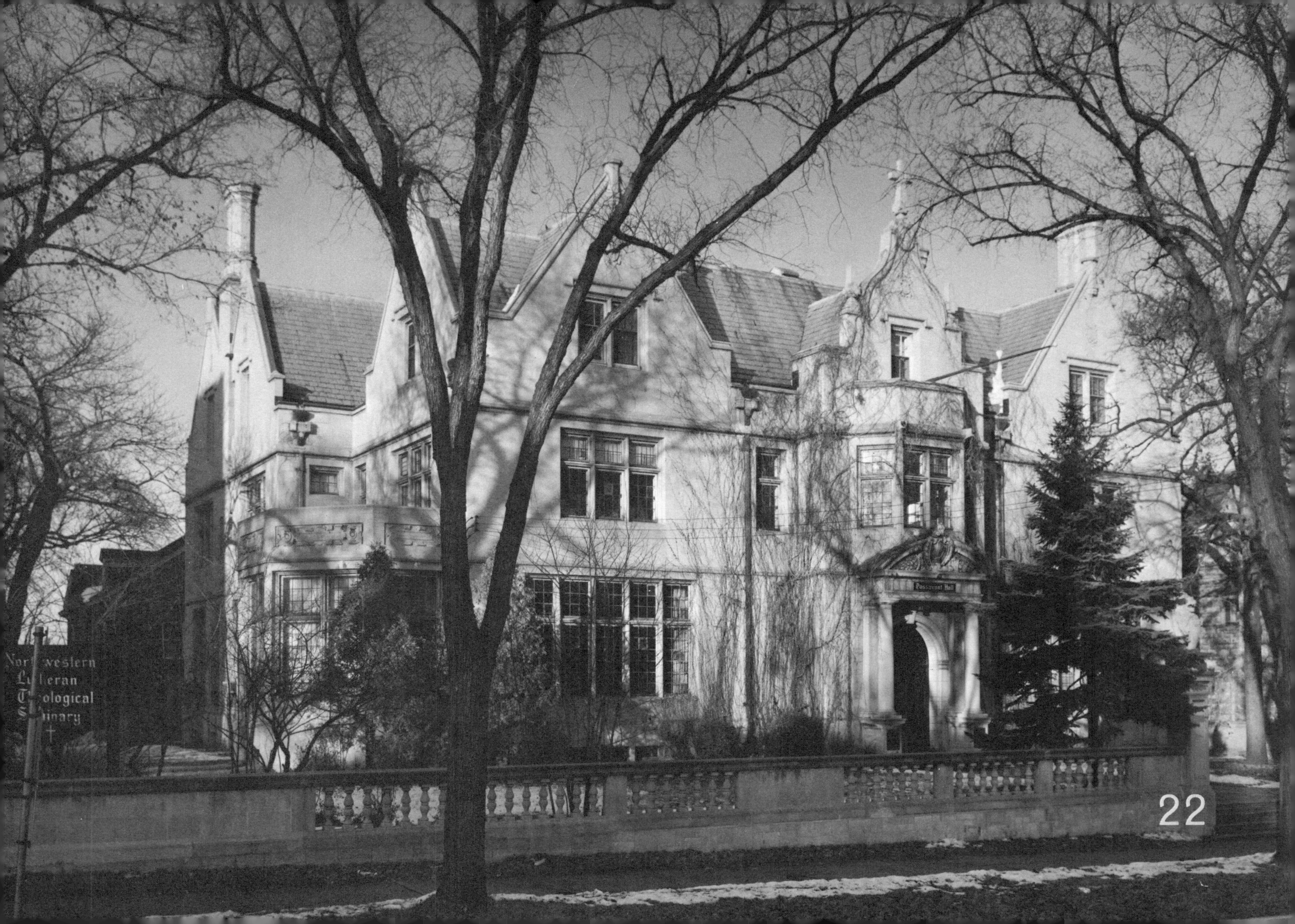

Passavant Hall
Northwestern
Lutheran
Theological
Seminary
22

Pittsburgh Plate Glass Co.   1910

(formerly Northern Implement Co.)

616 South 3rd Street

by Kees and Colburn (Minneapolis)

In this design Kees and Colburn used the same vocabulary of forms and motifs and the same design sources as were noted in their building for Deere and Weber of eight years earlier. (The number of buildings of the same general character by this firm is more extensive than is suggested in this list of buildings.) Here the sense of solidity and massiveness is even more emphatic because of the unbroken extent of the enframing wall that surrounds the arcades on the principal facades. Above a basement, or ground, story of dressed limestone the handsomely laid walls of purple brick again rise to a termination in the form of a slight, flaring curve, a blossoming. The subtlety of this terminal curve, like the precise, graduated chamfer of the brick at building corners, amplifies the sense of monumental dignity and permanence notable in several designs by Serenus H. Colburn (1871-1927). After fifty-five years, this building is, we believe, still the best designed commercial-industrial structure yet built in Minneapolis.

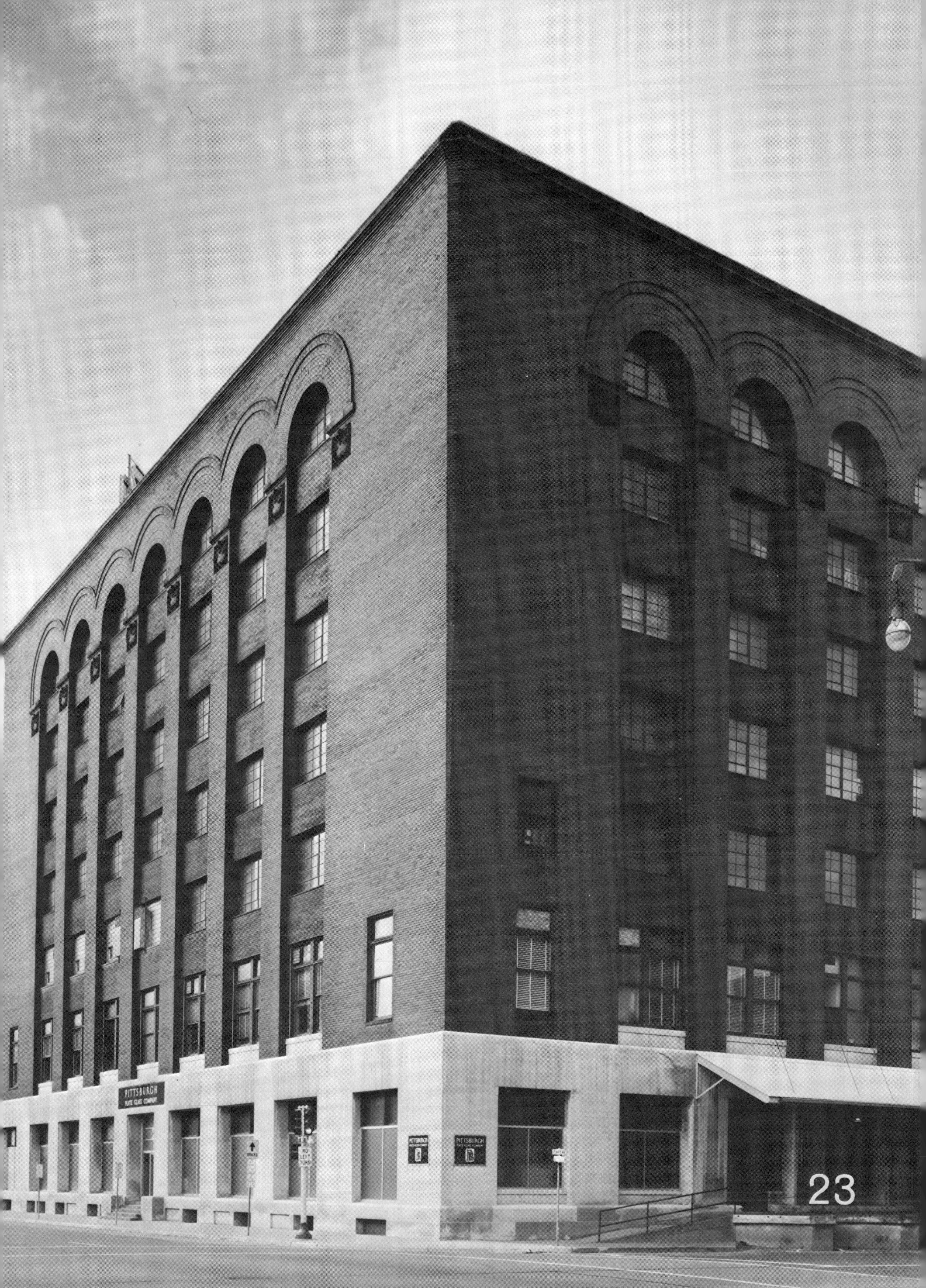

PITTSBURGH
PLATE GLASS COMPANY
PITTSBURGH
NO LEFT TURN

The Minneapolis Institute of Arts   1913-1915
201 East 24th Street
by McKim, Mead and White (New York)

The great variety of forms and motifs that had come to be accepted as parts of the Classic tradition came to a renewed popularity in the late eighties and soon were used on any and all types of building. But Classicism in general, and the columned portico in particular, continued to be thought of as particularly appropriate to buildings that served some ethical or cultural end, or that were meant to symbolize established values, stability and permanence. It is to that mode of thought that the Institute of Arts owes its general format, Roman portico and rotunda. Designs of the general type were turned out by the McKim, Mead and White office in considerable numbers and varied in quality from very good to poor. The Institute, unfortunately, is not one of the firm's most successful designs. It should be noted that the building is no more than a small, central fragment of the wildly grandiose and immense museum complex projected by the architects.

The very features, as monumental stairs and very high ceilings, that were meant to make the building impressive have made it difficult to use and the monumental scale of the exterior is out of accord with the interior spaces, many of which are ill adapted to the display of works of art. Despite all of that, the Institute does not lack dignity and it is not likely to be re-placed by a better building. Together with First Christian Church, the former Pillsbury residences, the Minneapolis Branch of the American Association of University Women, and the Hennepin County Historical Society, it does much to enhance the already handsome Fairoaks Park. Additions that are made to this perimeter of buildings around the park should be carefully controlled or the quality of the district will be destroyed.

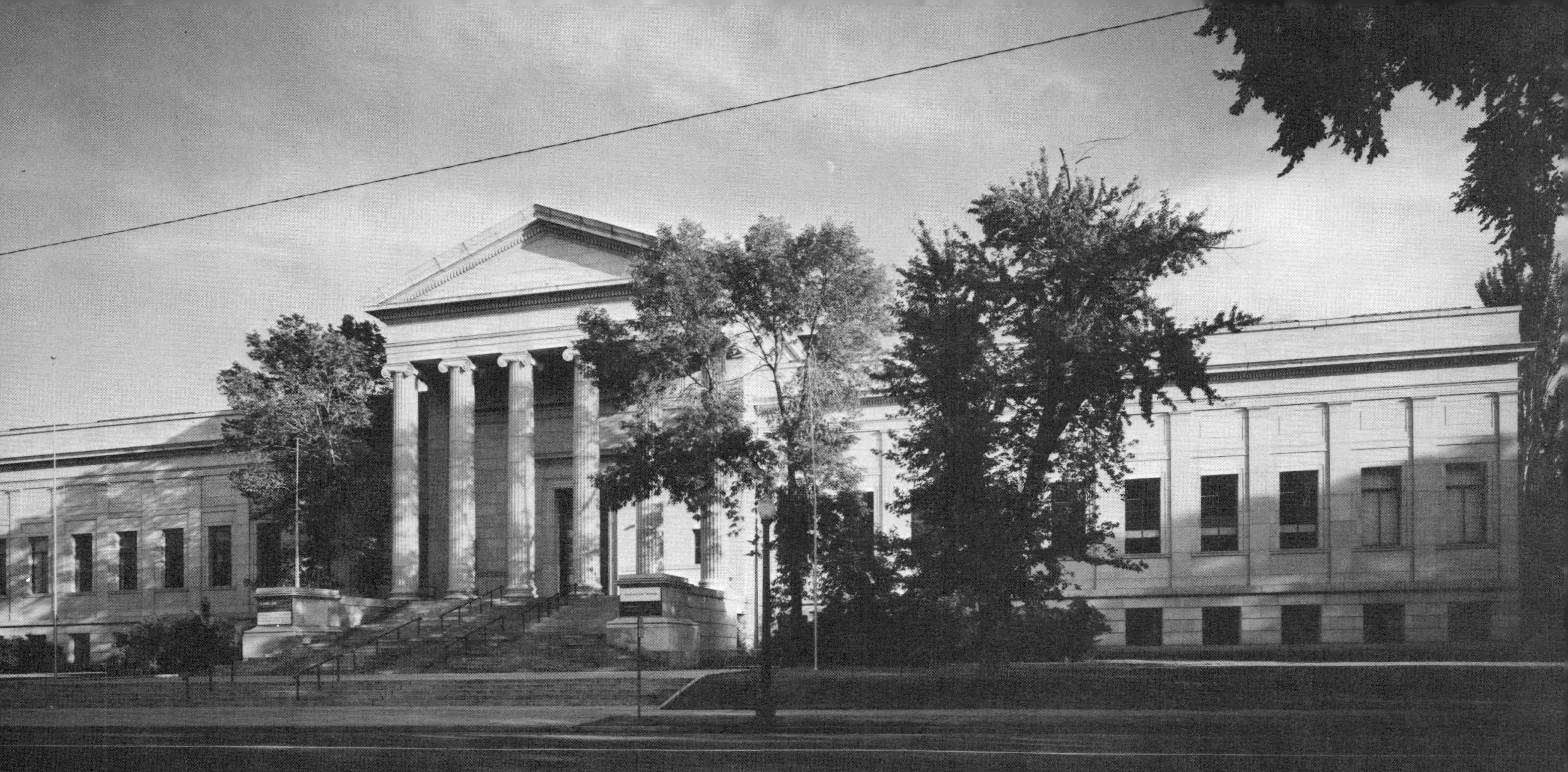

24

William Grey Purcell   1913

(now A.B. Cutts) residence

2328 Lake Place

   and

Dr. Oscar Owre   1911-12

(now E.H. Newhart) residence

2625 Newton Ave. South

by Purcell and Elmslie (Minneapolis)

Purcell and Elmslie maintained an office in Minneapolis for about a decade after 1908. Both subscribed fully to the beliefs about nature and architecture that Louis Sullivan and Frank Lloyd Wright considered the philosophical basis for their 'Organic' architecture. Purcell, who spent his youth in Oak Park, Illinois, knew Wright's fine early work while still a child. Elmslie held responsible positions in the Sullivan office for over twenty years.

Of the buildings (fifteen houses and one church) by Purcell and Elmslie in Minneapolis proper, all are worthy of attention. Now, more than a half-century after their construction they remain thoroughly 'Modern' designs. In the mode of their planning, in their use of materials, in their fenestration, the debt to the Sullivan-Wright 'tradition' is evident, but they are distinguished buildings in their own right, not to be dismissed as derivative. The interior spaces in the Lake Place residence merit comparison with the best of Wright's work; the simplicity and cohesion of the Newton Avenue South design are of an order seldom found in Minneapolis domestic architecture.

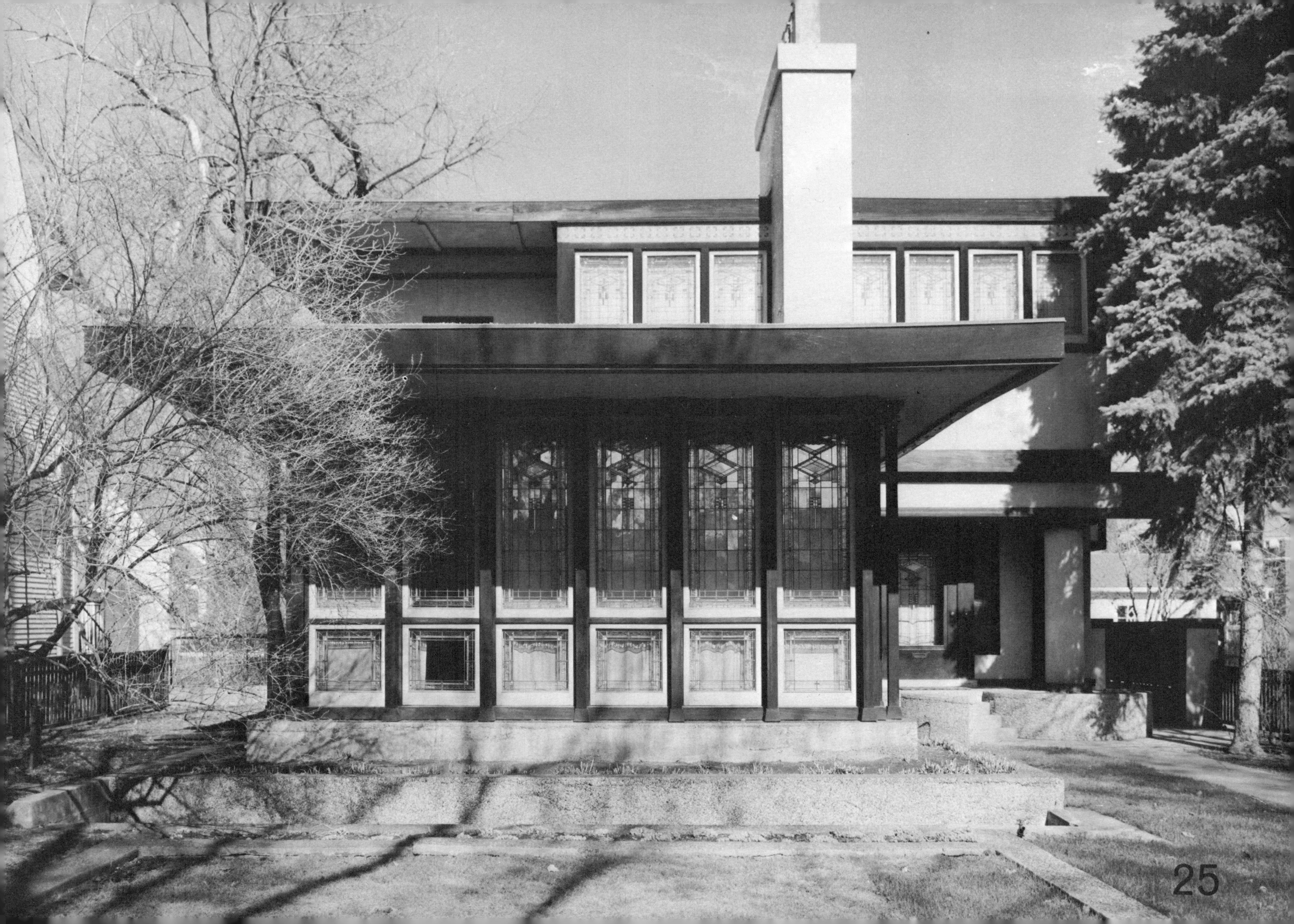

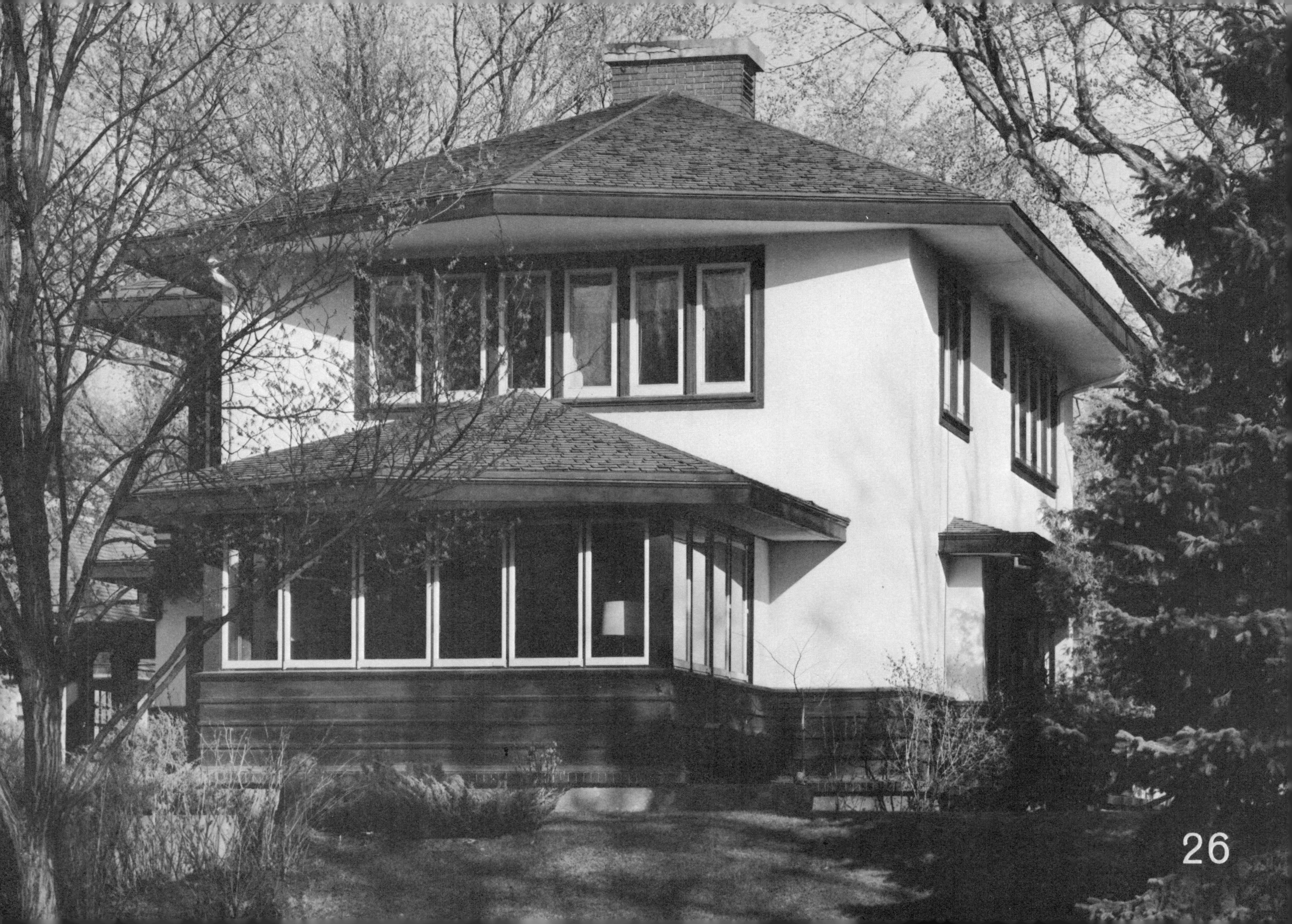
26

Christ Lutheran Church   1949-1950

3244 - 34th Avenue South

by Eliel and Eero Saarinen (Bloomfield Hills, Michigan)

Christ Lutheran Church is in Longfellow Community. While of
recent origin and certainly not in danger of demolition, it is
brought within this brief list of outstanding buildings not only
because it is a notably meritorious structure but because of its
extensive, and generally good, influence on church design and on
the acceptance of a "modern" idiom for church design in and
around Minneapolis. Christ Lutheran's quality stems from the
sensitive use of structural materials left in their natural state,
from their use and development in forms that attain proper
acoustical balance, from the quietly dramatic handling of natural
light to proclaim the essential purpose of the edifice, and from
the sense of spacious serenity that results from the conjunction
of these several carefully considered aspects of the building.

The church, like the warehouses and factory-assembly plants
cited above, is strikingly lacking in the pretense, the empty
rhetoric, which has continued to characterize so much of our
architecture.

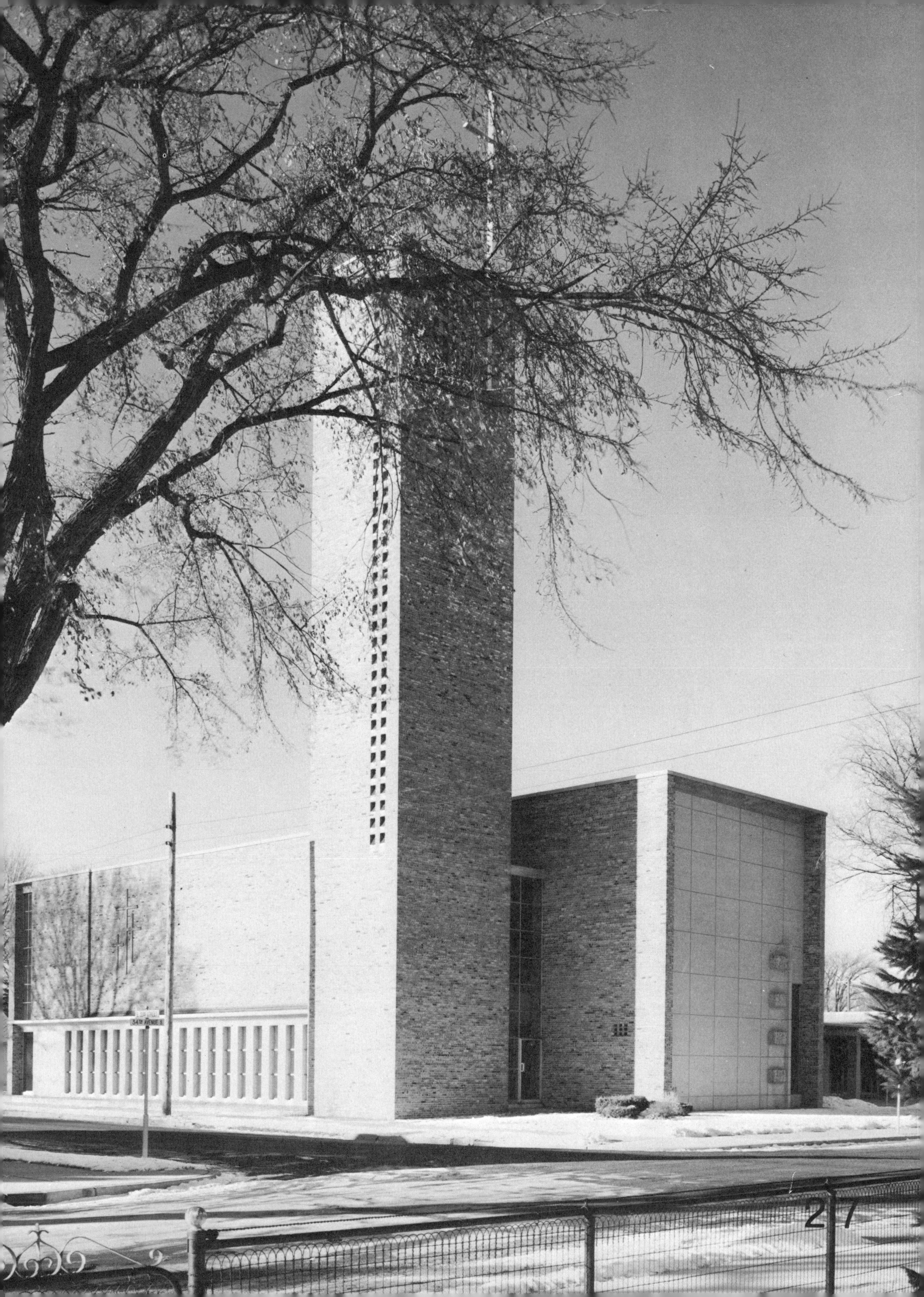

Malcolm Willey (now Burris) residence   1934

255 Bedford Street SE

<u>and</u>

Henry Neils residence   1951

2815 Burnham Boulevard

by Frank Lloyd Wright (Spring Green)

Earliest among the several buildings that Wright designed for
Minnesota is the very large and handsome house (1913) for F.W.
Little (now Stevenson) at Northome on Lake Minnetonka.

Next, in point of time was that for Malcolm Willey in 1934. It
is quite small, complex and subtle in the modulation of its spaces
and the relations among its parts--an outstanding example of the
small house type Wright called 'Usonian.' The somewhat more ex-
pansive Neils house, built seventeen years later, is equally complex and more dramatic, but not superior to the designs of earlier
date.

In both of the examples within the city Wright exploited the
potentials of building site with his customary brilliance, employed
unusual materials with great skill, in the earlier example--
Milwaukee sewer brick, in the later--quarry 'trimmings' of Minnesota
marble; in both the design potential of natural light is employed
with a brilliance seldom, if ever, encountered in the work of
Wright's contemporaries.

Many of Wright's great and revolutionary designs have not
fared well in recent years. If the need to do so should arise, it
is to be hoped that Minneapolis can accord these houses the same
respect as is paid them by their owners.

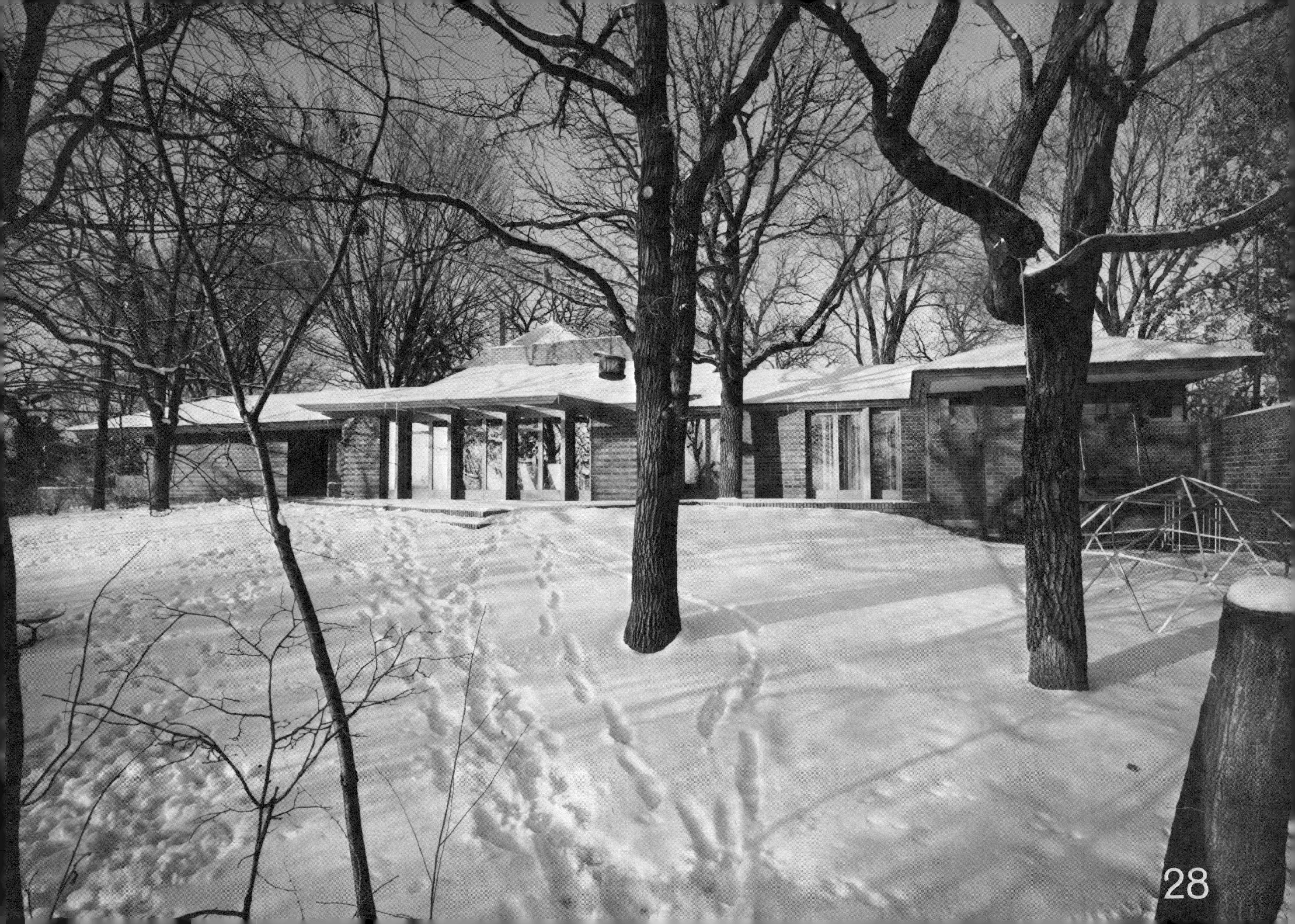

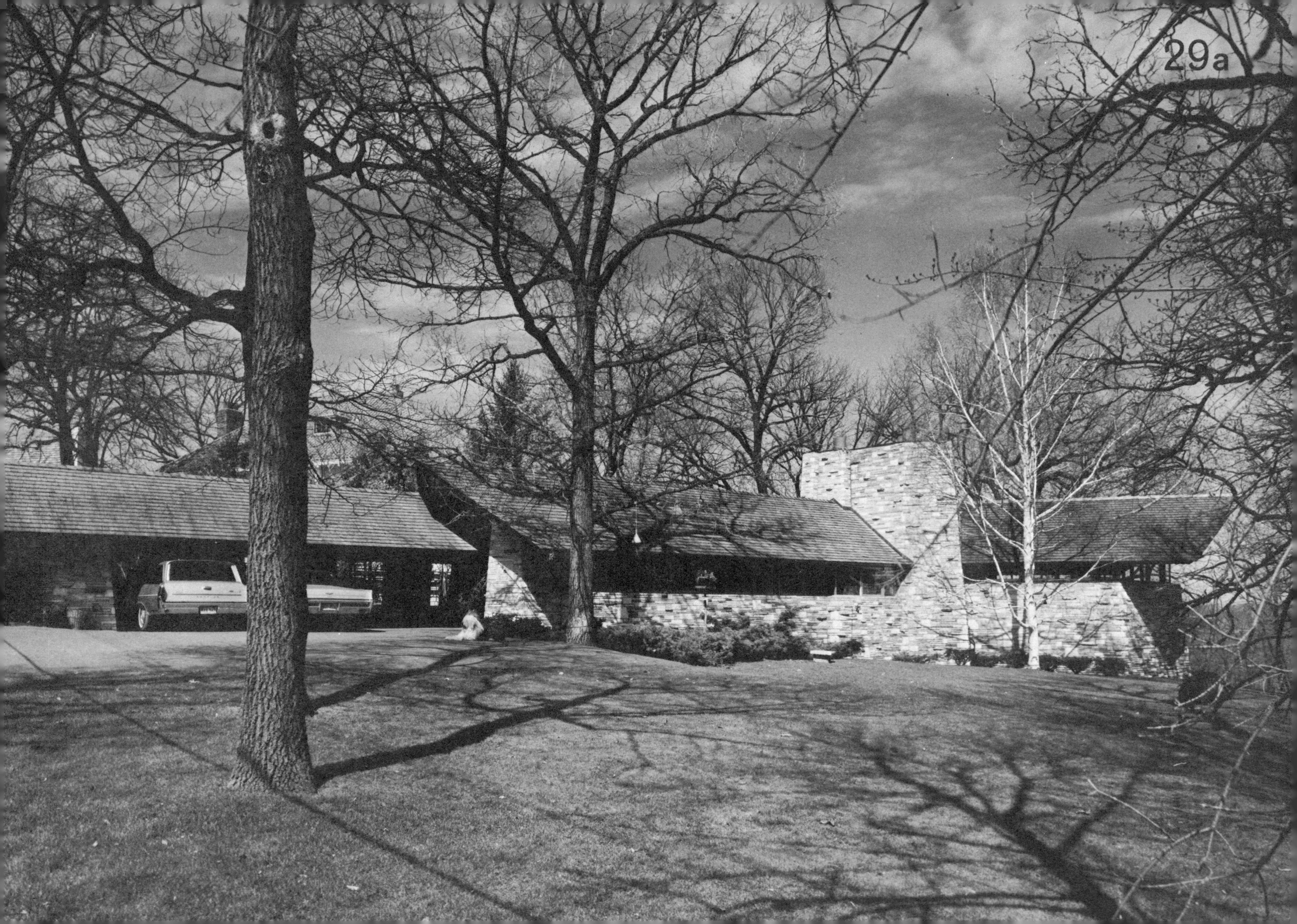

29a

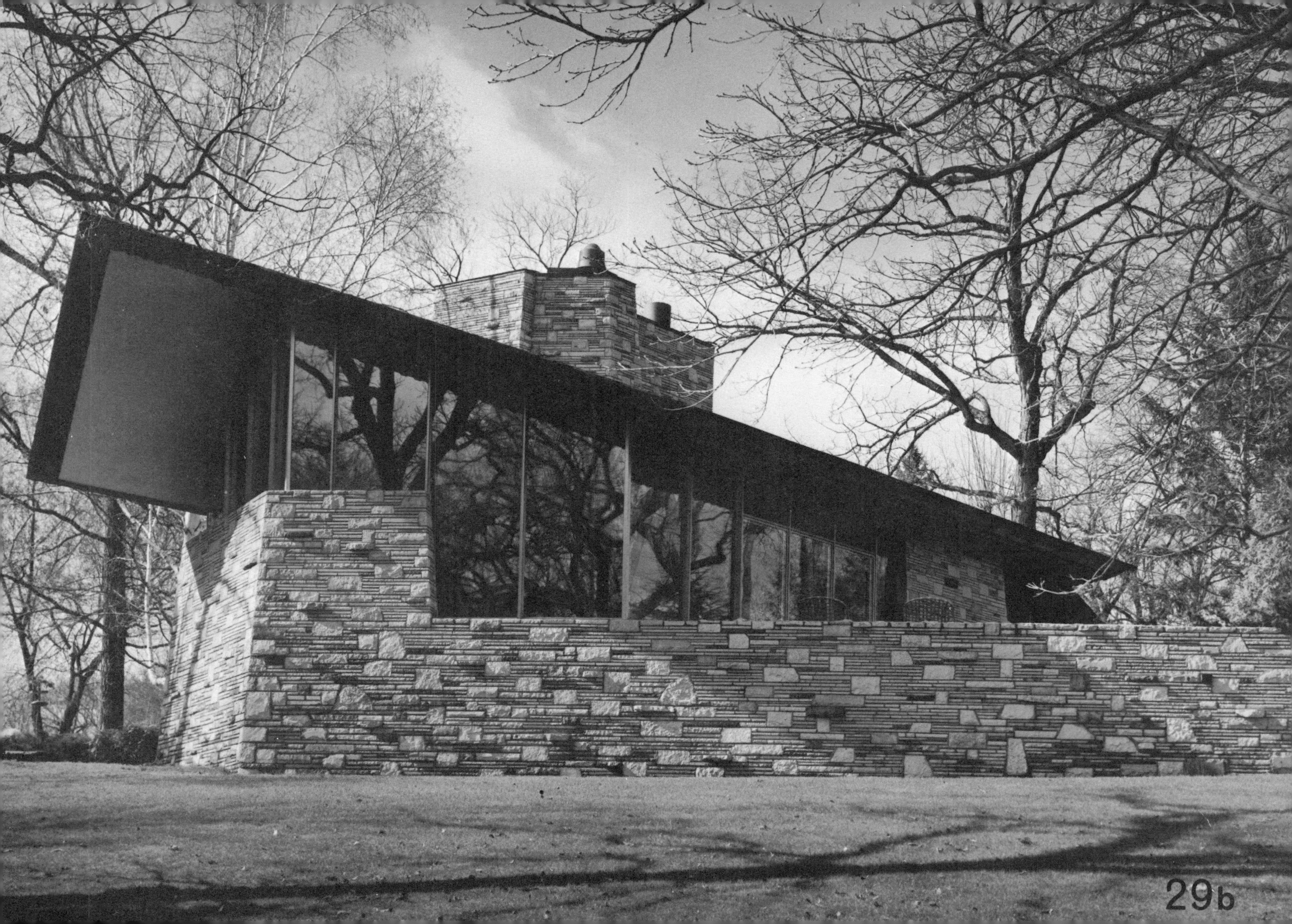

Some of the most interesting and most significant structures in and around the city belong more properly to the field of engineering than to that of architecture. They are the bridges and grain storage elevators.

The river was spanned by a bridge as early as 1855, but the earliest among several truly splendid examples is the stone bridge designed for the St. Paul, Minneapolis and Manitoba railroad by Colonel Charles L. Smith, of 1881-84. In the splendid series of catenary arches each block of the rock-faced granite or limestone is shaped and placed to express its structural role. It is one of the region's great masonry constructions. (Illustrations 30a, 30b)

That early example was followed, between 1917 and 1929, by four fine bridges in reinforced concrete--the Third Avenue Bridge (1917-1918) (Illustration 31), the Cappelen Memorial (Franklin Avenue) (1919-1925) (Illustration 32), the Mendota (1923-1924) and the Cedar Avenue (1923-1929). Among these several, Walter S. Wheeler's Mendota Bridge and the Cappelen Memorial excited and merited attention beyond this region by reason of their size and the grace of their design.

Among the increasing number of people who are interested in conservation and preservation of buildings and landmarks for historical or esthetic reasons, a substantial number look with antipathy on change of any kind. They are not necessarily committed blindly to the past; when the bridges cited above, of the period 1880-1930, are compared with the recently completed Washington Avenue and Dartmouth Avenue bridges it is easy to understand--if not to subscribe to--the fear that anything out of the past which is destroyed is almost certain to be replaced by

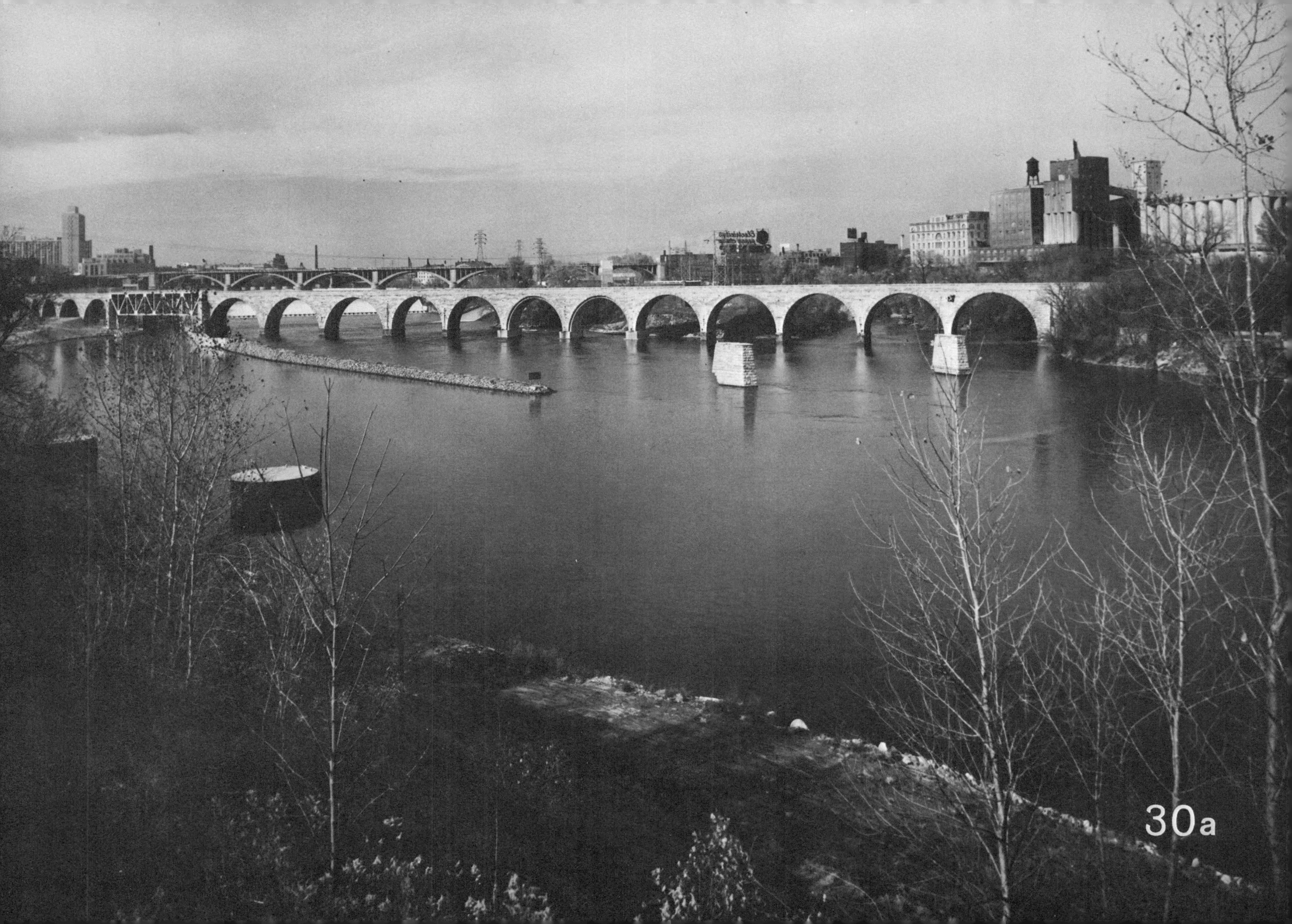

30a

ugliness. Careless, thoughtless, ill-considered demolition must be stopped in the general social interest, but to demand that everything out of the past be saved is irresponsible folly.

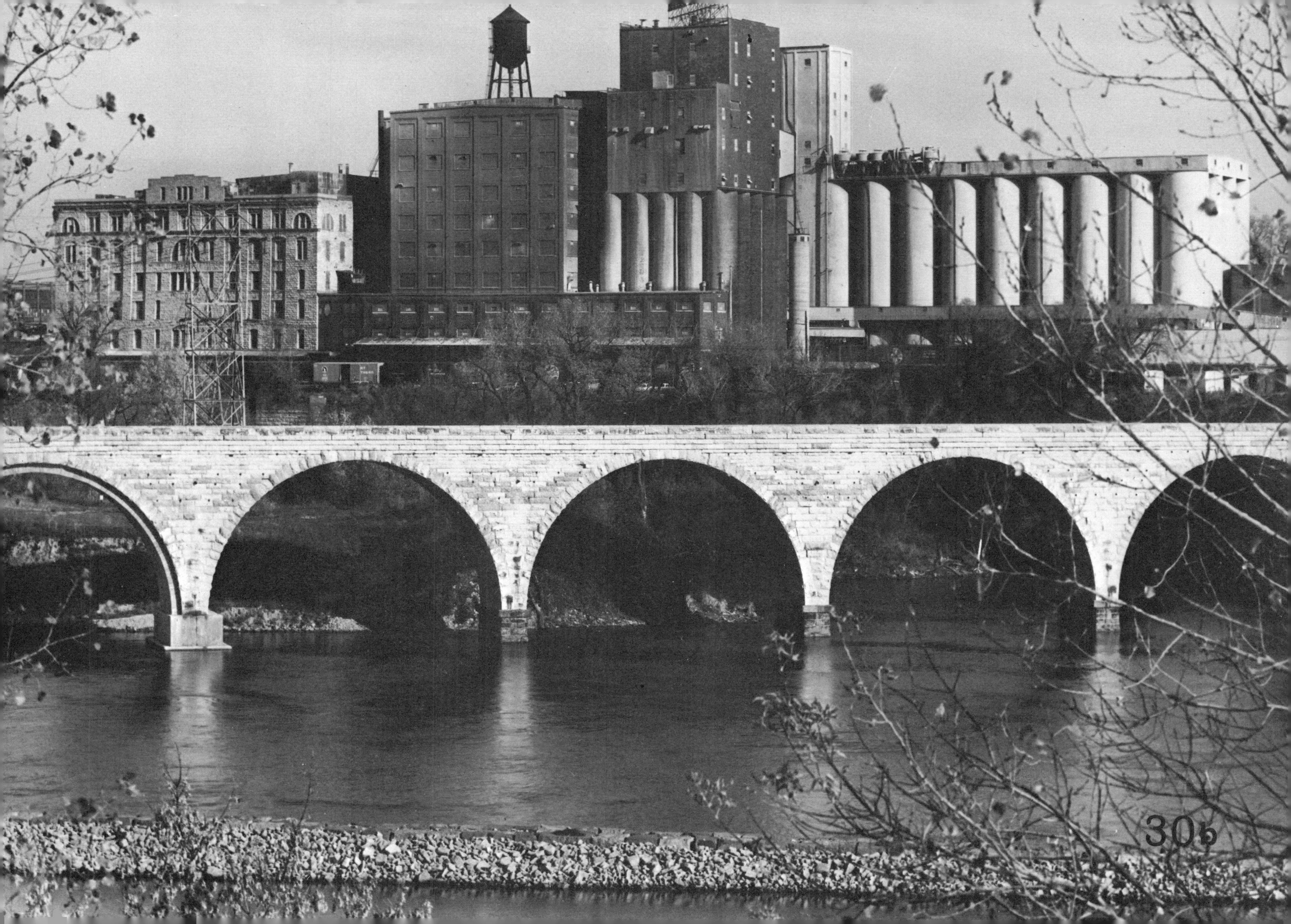

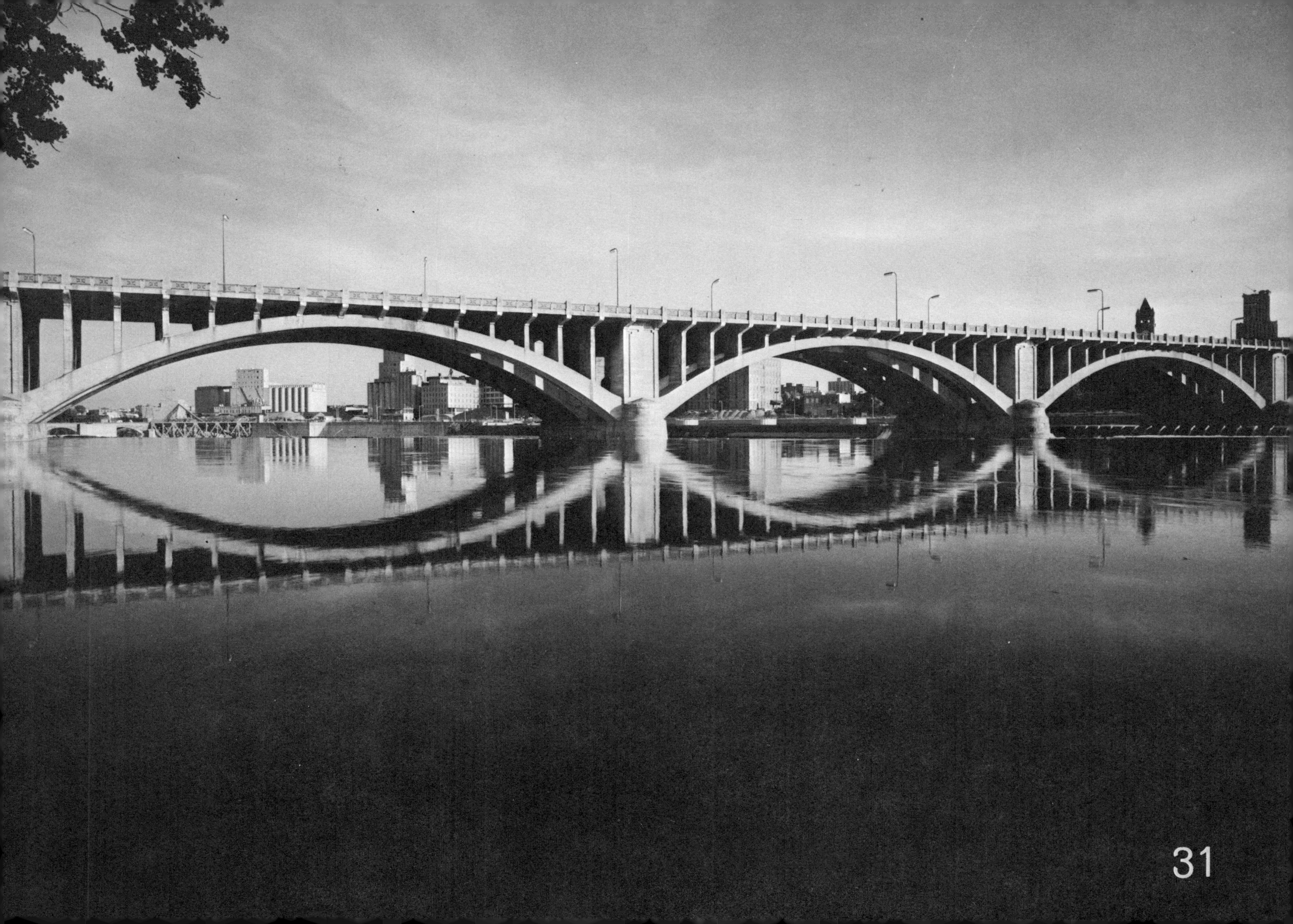

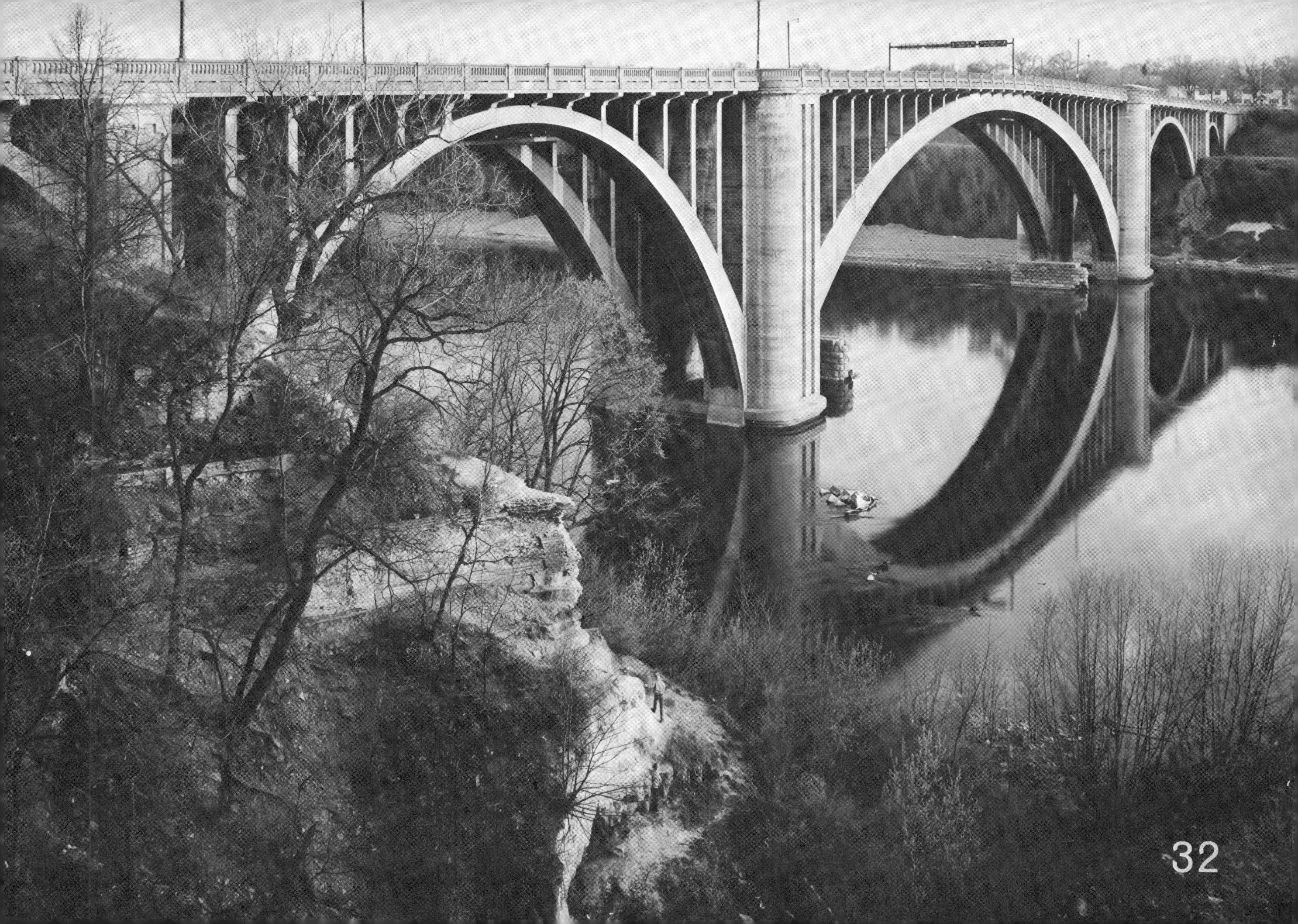

The grain storage elevators vary widely in the quality of their design. Groups that are impressively massed and handsomely proportioned are seen in close association with Pillsbury "A" Mill, near General Mills--in their No.2 (1916-1929) on 2nd Street at 10th Avenue South. (Illustration 33) Others, independent of visual association with mills are in the railroad yards of Southeast Minneapolis, as--the Archer Daniels Midland group at 29th Ave. S.E. and the Chicago and Great Western tracks (Illustration 34), or those near Highway 7 beyond the west side limits of the city. The most truly historical among the many elevators--first successful round, concrete, grain storage bin in America, built in 1899-1900 as a test case for the Peavey Co.--stands beyond the city limits near Highway 7 at Highway 100, where it has been relegated to the role of a signboard for Lumber Stores, Inc. Properly cared for, any of these structures are cmmunity assets.

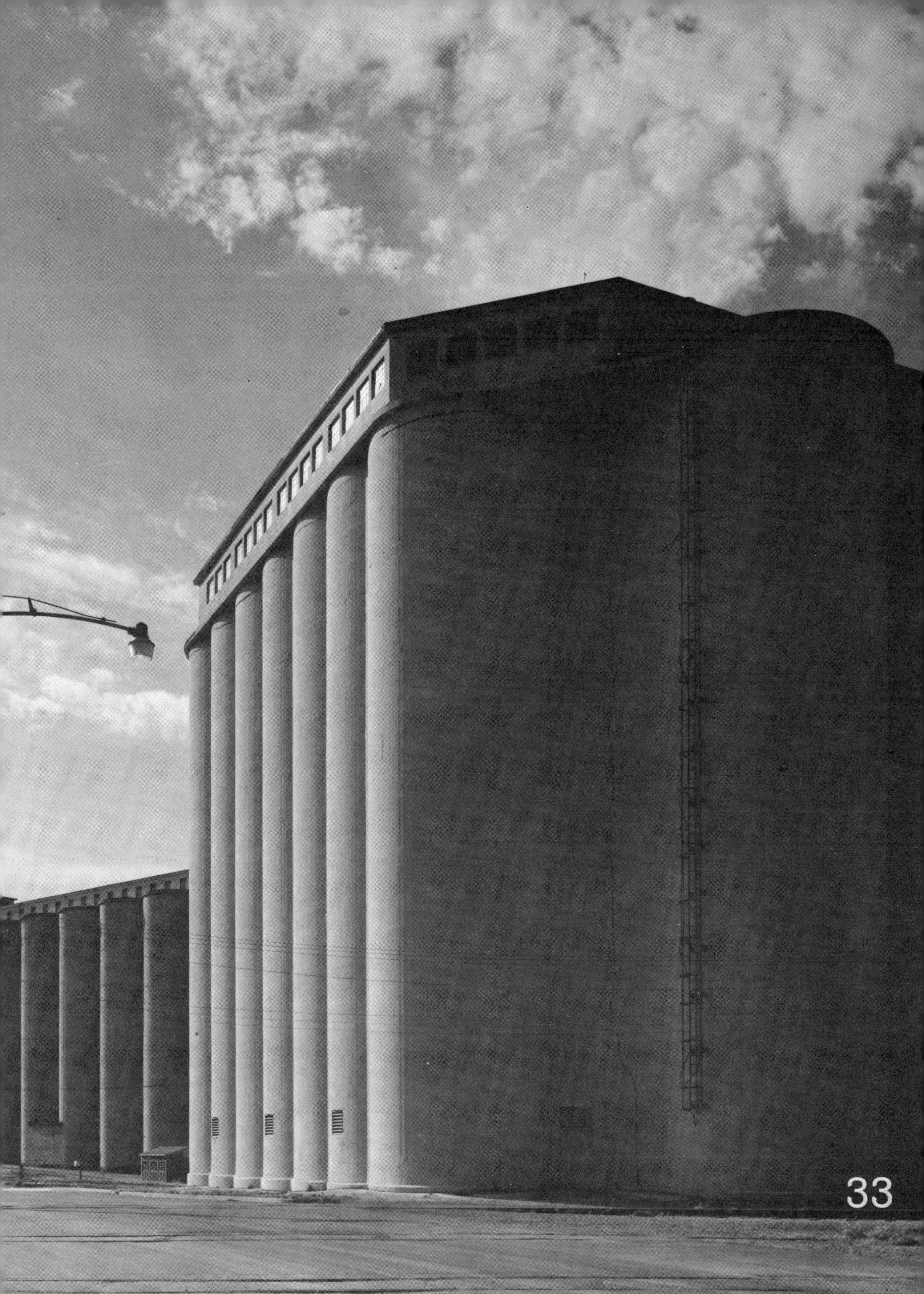

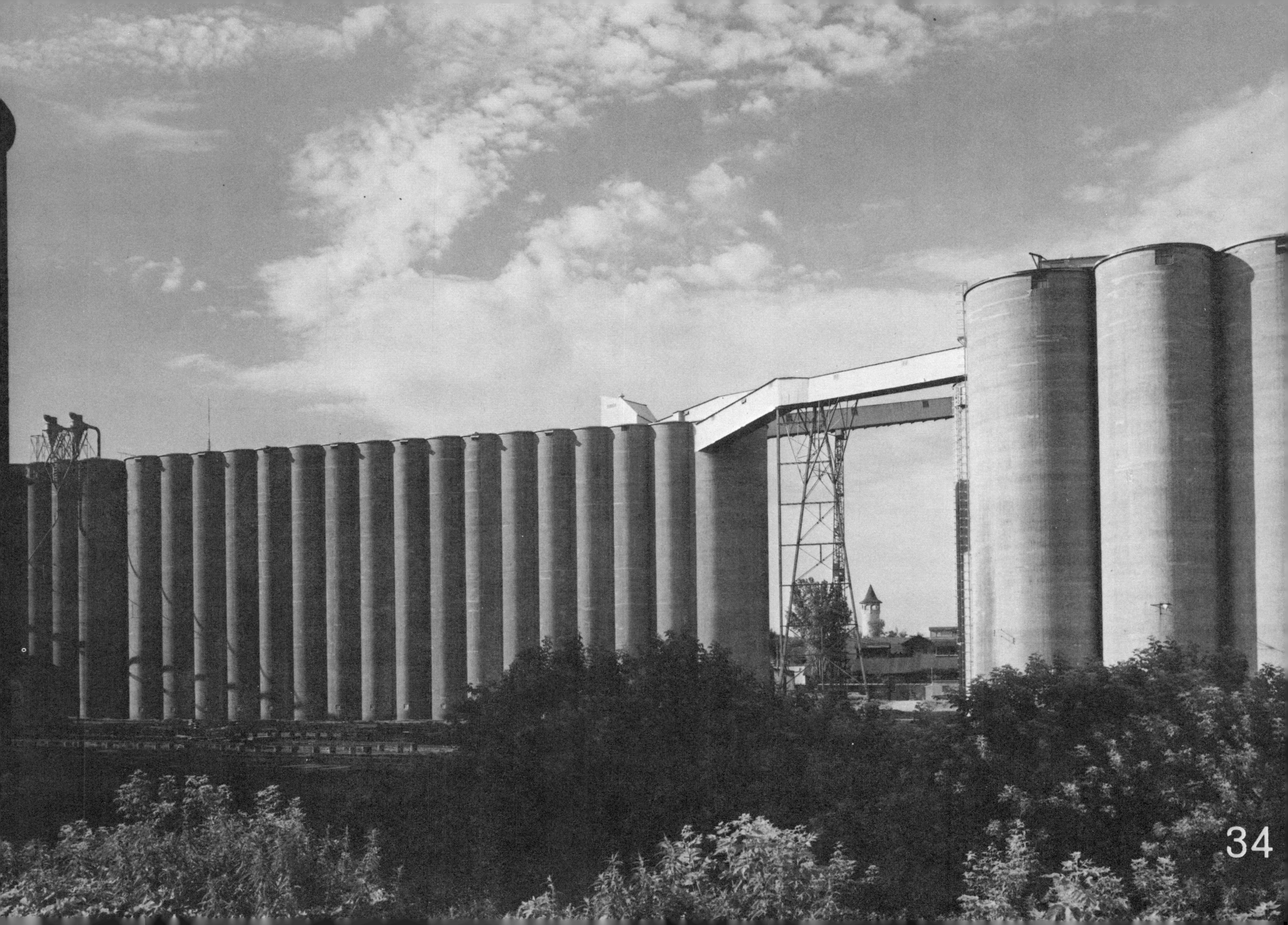

As was noted above, the brevity of this list of structures should not be understood to mean that no others within the area are considered worthy of attention, conservation or preservation. Of building completed in very recent years, the following should be noted: In 1956 the Minnesota Society of Architects, A.I.A. initiated an annual awards program for projects designed by architects licensed to practice in Minnesota. Projects submitted by their authors are judged by a jury of distinguished architects from outside the region who may, when they wish, cite a project for Honor Award, Merit Award or Honorable Mention. In the course of eleven years, one hundred and seventeen awards have been made, a substantial number for buildings in Minneapolis suburbs, but only eighteen of the citations are for buildings within the city limits. They are:

First Christian Church 2201 First Avenue South	Honor Award	1957 Thorshov & Cerny, Inc.
American Hardware Mutual Ins. Co. 3033 Excelsior Blvd.	Honor Award	1957 Thorshov & Cerny, Inc.
St. Mary's Greek Orthodox Church 3450 Irving Avenue South	Honor Award	1958 Thorshov & Cerny, Inc.
Northwestern Hospital Power Plant & Laundry Building 810 East 27th Street	Merit Award	1958 Magney, Tusler, & Setter
Lutheran Welfare Society Building 2414 Park Avenue	Merit Award	1958 Sovik, Mathre & Assoc.
Minneapolis School of Art Addition 200 East 25th Street	Honor Award	1959 Magney, Setter, Leach, Lindstrom & Erickson
Lyndale Homes Housing Project Lyndale Avenue North--Olson Highway	Honor Award	1960 Thorshov & Cerny

Golden Age Homes, Housing for
  the Elderly
Eleventh Avenue North--Bryant--
  Dupont
	Honorable Mention	1961
		Elizabeth & Winston Close

Harrison Elementary School Addition James and Fourth Avenues North	Honorable Mention 1961 S.C. Smiley and Assoc.
The Church of the Holy Name 3637 -Eleventh Avenue South	Honor Award 1962 The Cerny Assoc., Inc.
Sons of Norway Cultural & Bus. 1455 West Lake Street Center	Merit Award 1962 Thorsen & Thorshov, Inc.
School of Architecture Bldg. University, East Bank -Church Street	Merit Award 1962 The Cerny Assoc., Inc.
Benjamin A. Gingold, Jr. Res. 4745 Girard Avenue South	Special Merit Award 1962 Benjamin Gingold, AIA
Tyrone Guthrie Theatre 725 Vineland Place	Honor Award 1963 Ralph Rapson AIA, Architect

University Office for the State
Capitol Credit Union (Now Mpls.
  Public Library Branch)
4th Street and Thirteenth Avenue
  SE
	Honor Award 1964
	Ralph Rapson, AIA,
	Architect Inc.

Werness Brothers Funeral Chapel 3500 West 50th Street	Honorable Mention 1964 Thorsen & Thorshov, Inc.
Alpha Gamma Delta Sorority House 401 - Eleventh Avenue SE	Honorable Mention 1965 Roger Johnson, Architect
Social Science - Humanities Building University - West Bank Campus	Honorable Mention 1965 The Cerny Assoc., Inc.

Minneapolis must make the decisions that will shape the future character of the city through its buildings, parks and highways, and these decisions lie in the immediate future. If there is real desire to preserve the good and meaningful out of the past, and desire to direct the quality of future work to higher levels, people must plan for it, work for it, and pay for it. It will not come about in any other way.

———

FINIS

The preparation of this report was financed in part through
a Community Renewal Program Grant from the U.S. Department of
Housing & Urban Development under the provisions of Section
103(d) of the Housing Act of 1949 as amended.

This study has been financed in part by generous contributions
from the Archie D. and Bertha H. Walker Foundation, The Minneapolis Foundation, the Honeywell Fund and Minneapolis Chapter,
American Institute of Architects.

Dr. Torbert gratefully acknowledges Grants in Aid of Research
awarded to him by the Graduate School of The University of
Minnesota.

Cover design by Mr. Peter Seitz
